Trippy Training Data

Image collection for this book took place during the COVID-19 pandemic quarantine of 2020-21. Reddit users' names have been abbreviated to preserve the anonymity of the community. Special thanks to Anisa Suthayalai, Alexandra Ching, and Natalie Kerby for design and copy guidance.

UNKNOWN UNKNOWNS
New York, NY
unknownunknowns.org

ISBN 978-0-9913923-6-0

Introduction

Training data is a collection of labeled information that is used to build a machine learning model. It can consist of annotated text, images, video, or audio. Through training data, an algorithm is programmed to perform a specific task, such as recognizing faces in photos or identifying cancerous lesions in x-rays. In order for a model to execute a new classification task, a programmer develops an algorithm using a large amount of relevant training data.

We encounter training data all the time. One example is the grid of images that pop up when we are just about to hit "submit" on a web form. When we click on all of the squares that contain a motorcycle or traffic light, we are creating training data. These labeled images will be applied to a machine learning algorithm so that a computer, like one operating a self-driving car, might one day be able to detect motorcycles and traffic lights on its own.

Training data can be acquired anywhere on the web. For instance, Reddit.com's online forums, subreddits, are often used as training data. These millions of posts are an excellent resource for natural language processing tasks like sentiment analysis, where algorithms are trained to recognize if review text is positive or negative, and predictive text, where an email application might guess how we are going to compose a sentence.

The images in this book are collected from the subreddit r/LSD, a community of people who share their questions and experiences with taking LSD. Posts in this subreddit include people asking for advice on dosage and sharing their original psychedelic art. Some people attempt to capture their hallucinatory visions using the shoddy cameras on their smartphones. These images are often of mundane objects, such as cold pizza and bathroom floor tiles. They are snapped under drab, fluorescent lighting and captioned in all caps with expressions like, "HOLY SHIT!"

Normally these images might belong to a collection of butt dial artifacts that get discarded to save space. However, the captions demand that we inspect the images more closely. Why are these photos worthy of such proclamations? If we stare long enough at marbled cheese as we go about our day, can we too experience something sublime?

When a programmer inputs labeled data into their algorithm, the resulting model generalizes rules, establishes relationships, and finds patterns–even if there are not any meaningful ones to be found. In his book, *Beyond One and Zero: Machines, Psychedelics, and Consciousness*, Andrew Smart theorizes that for computers to make better decisions, they need to also be trained to have subjective qualities like a sense of humor or tripping on acid. His reasoning is that learning these human perceptions, even faulty ones, would guide a machine learning model to make more fair decisions. Otherwise, calculations without human nuance might lead to overly optimized and inhumane results.

While Smart makes a novel point, training a computer to trip might be challenging. Tripping is a more complex process than the association of images and labels, as this book suggests. Providing a model thousands of images that are captioned with the word "Bruh" will teach a computer to identify other images that have the qualities of "Bruh," not to hallucinate.

For now, these images can instead train humans to imagine hallucinations when looking at everyday things in their home. The next time you are staring at your bathroom rug, you might adapt to this new perspective and think to yourself "What the fu k."

–Angie Waller

☞

Dataset

Posted by u/vito**** 2 days ago

16

Currently Tripping **Wow! Those fractals duude**

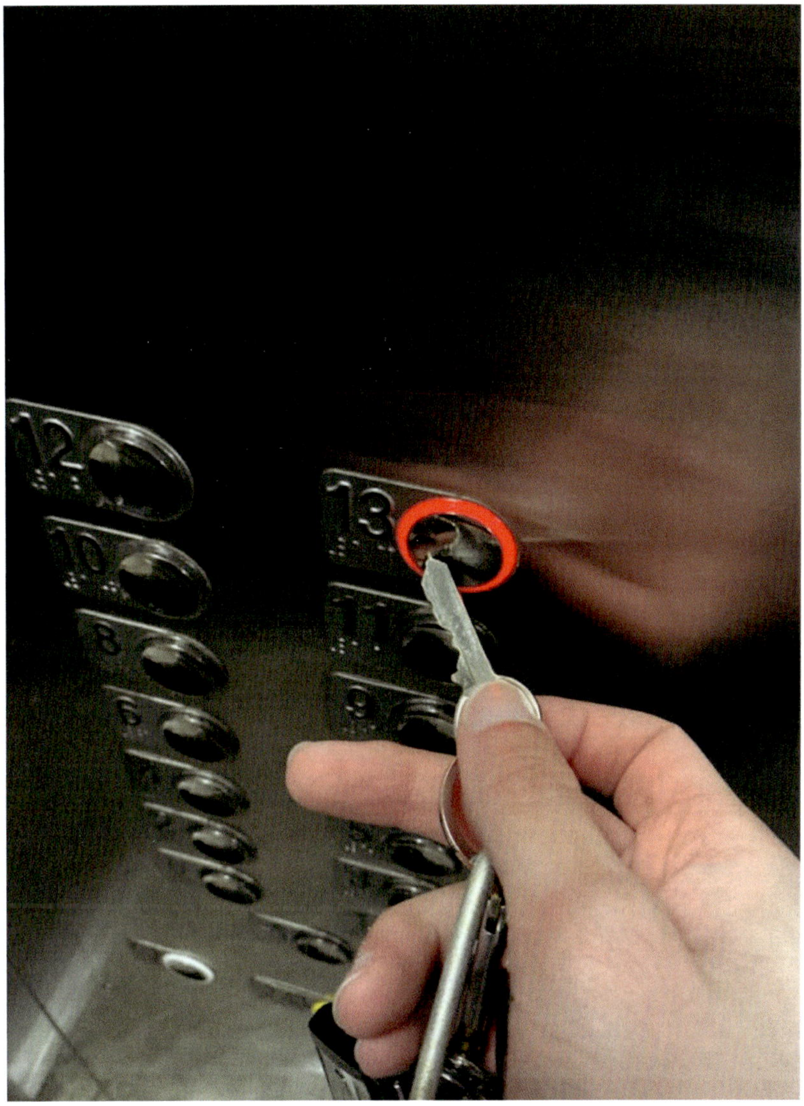

Posted by u/NotA**** 2 days ago

16

Currently Tripping **pizza on the plate**

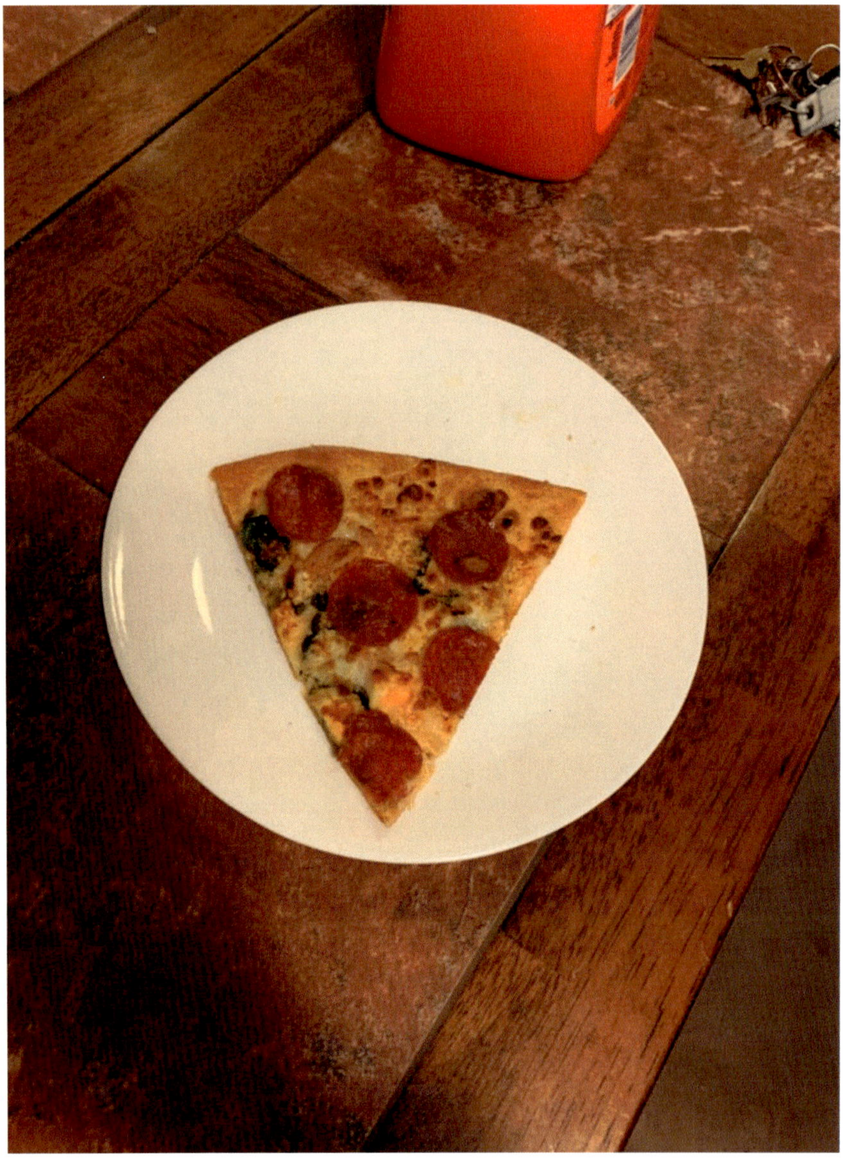

31

Posted by u/alej**** 2 days ago

Artwork **I did this with a beet, see the elephant?**

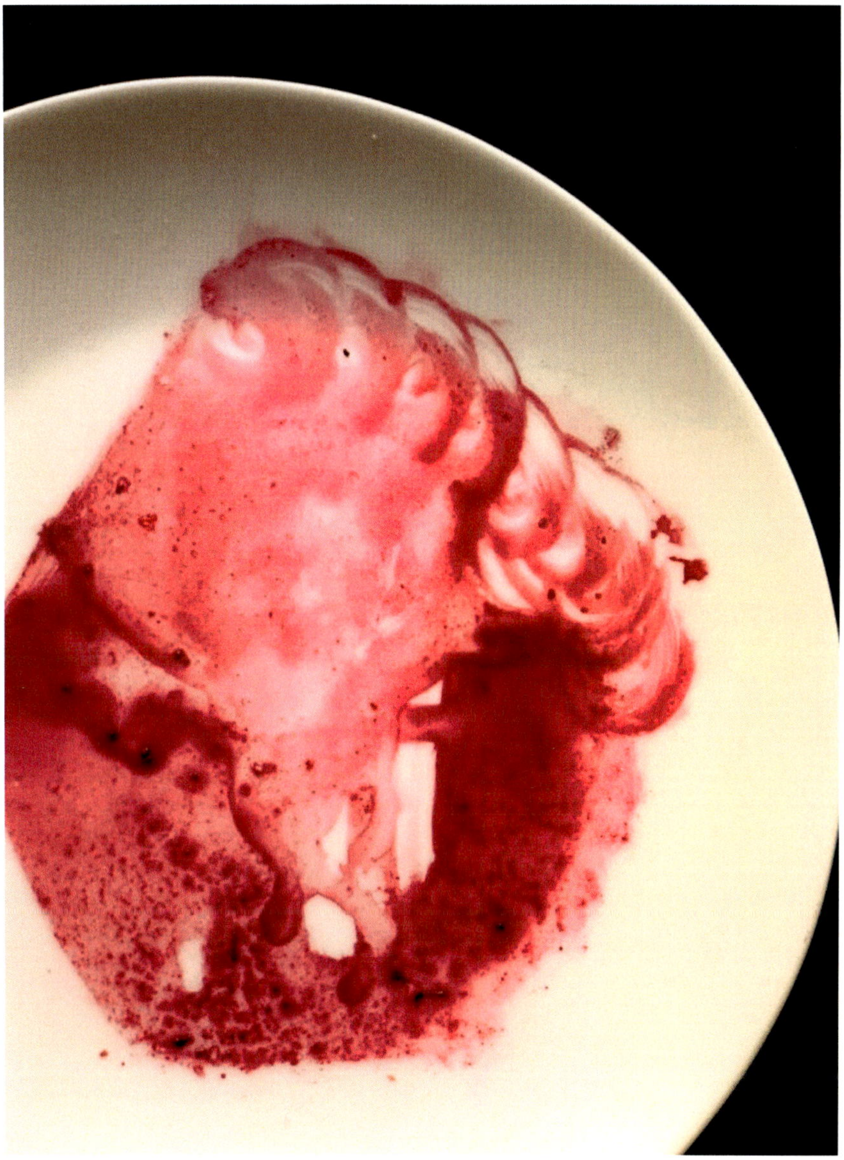

283

Posted by u/pelv**** 2 days ago

Currently Tripping **Holy shit**

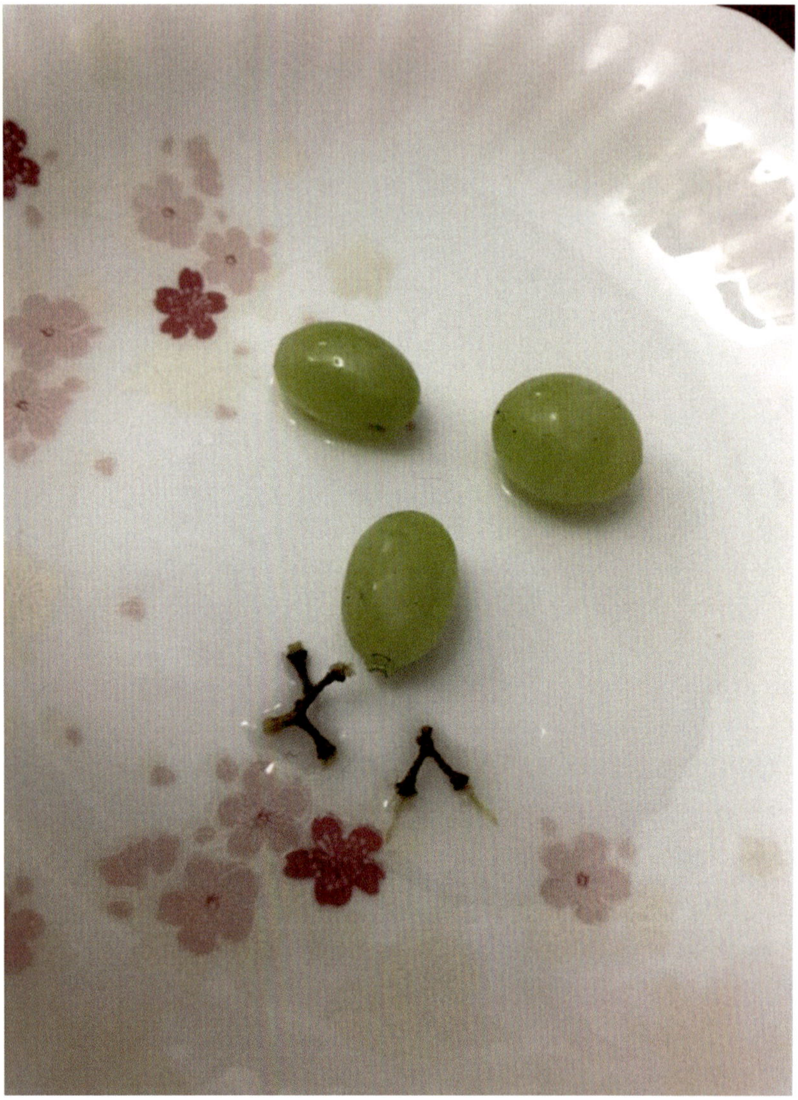

Posted by u/corn**** 2 days ago

23

WOW

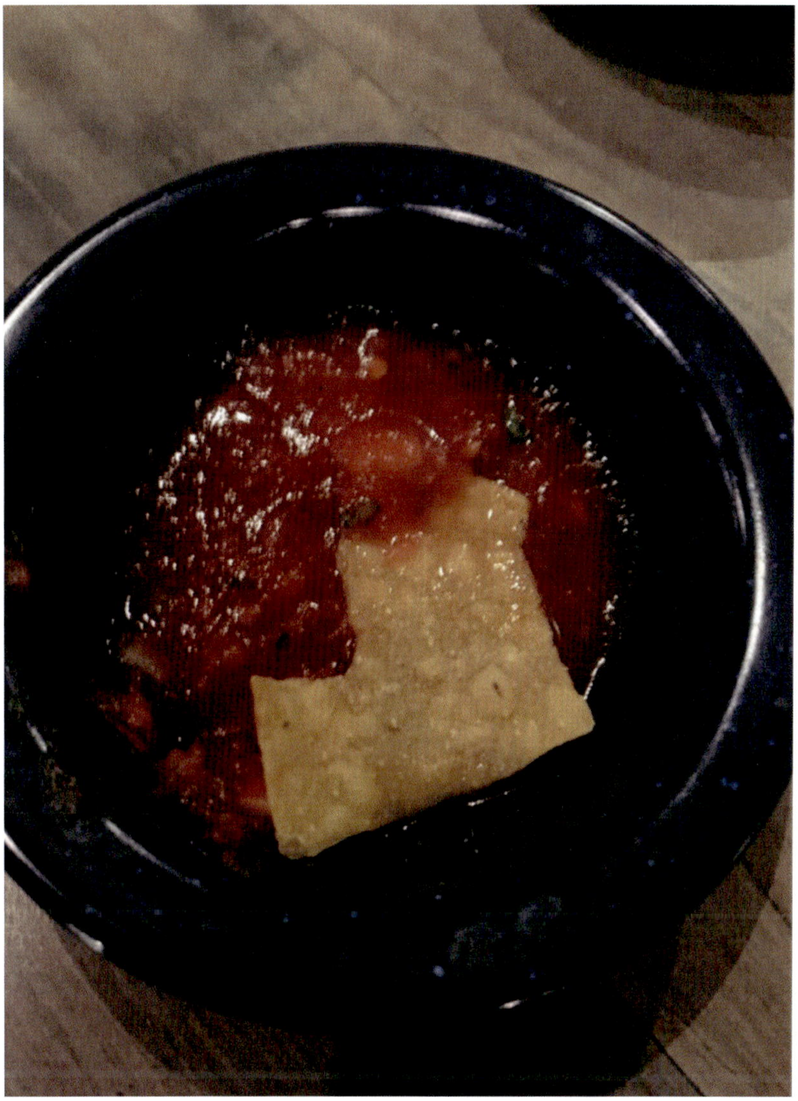

⬆ Posted by u/Twer**** 2 days ago

10

⬇ ✌ Currently Tripping ✌ **Woah**

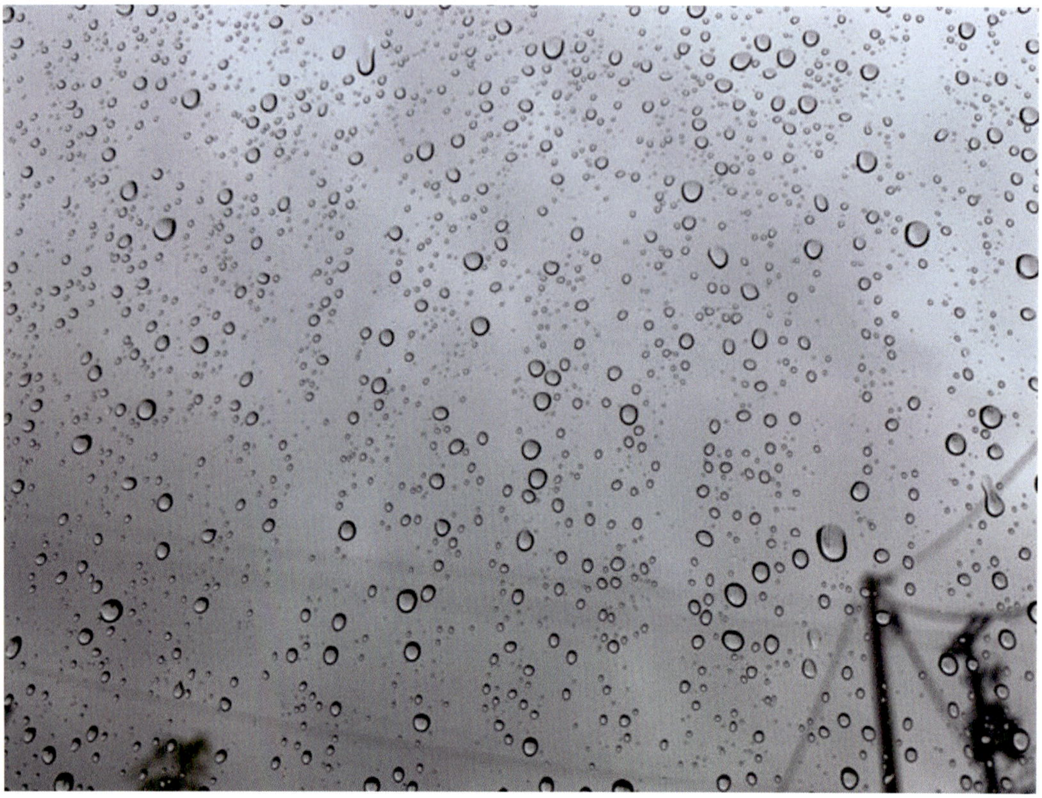

⬆ Posted by u/Wood**** 3 days ago
454
⬇ Currently Tripping **Woah.**

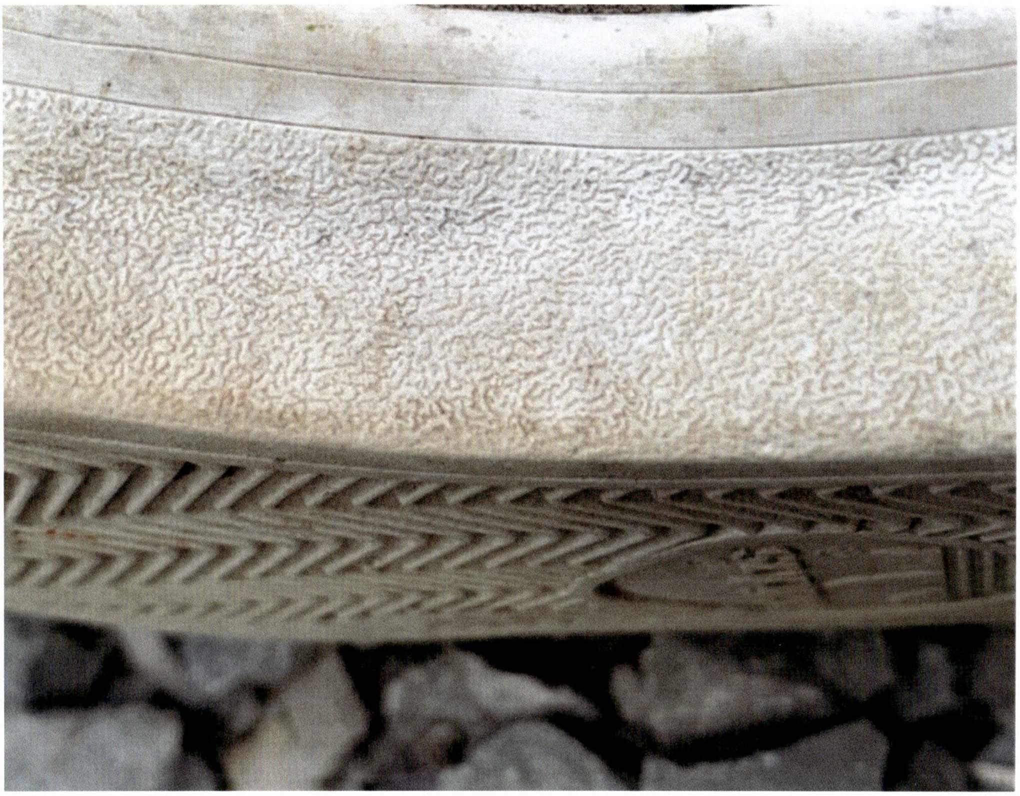

⬆ Posted by u/Papa**** 5 days ago

102

⬇ Nature trip **Woah**

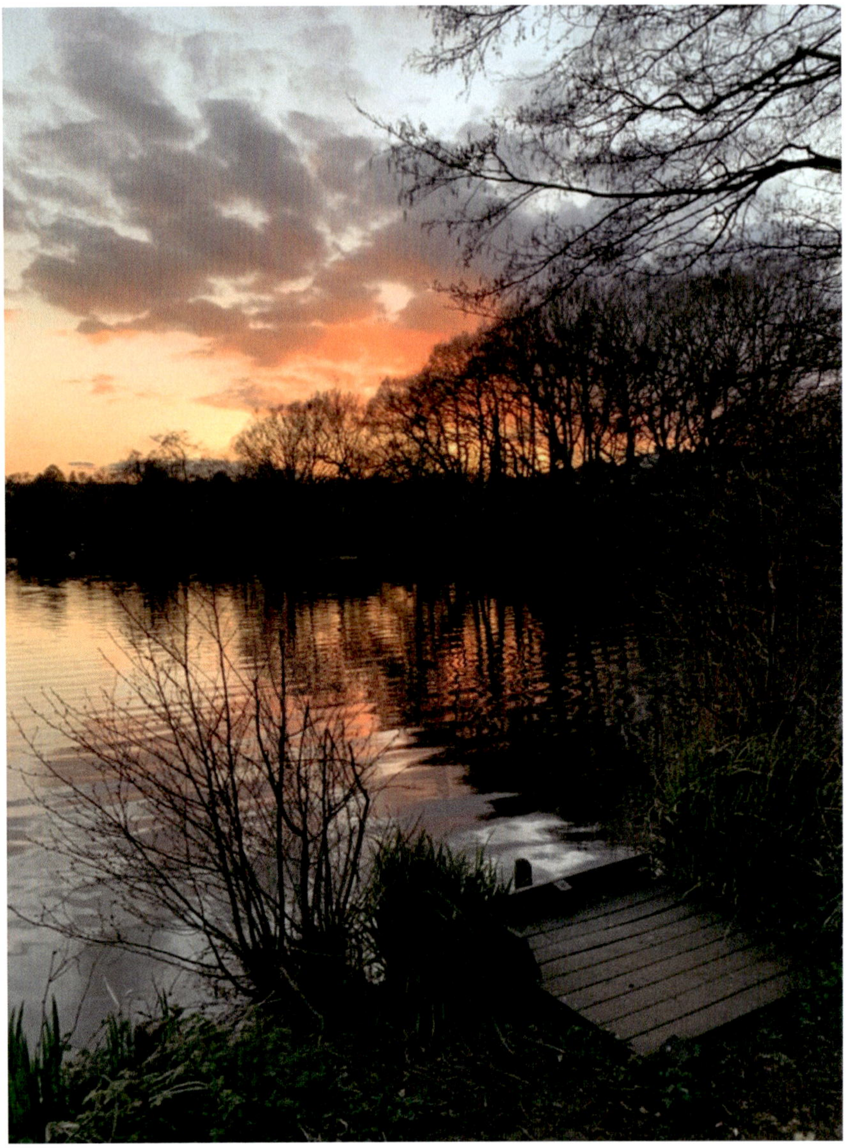

Posted by u/bipp**** 1 day ago

9

uh

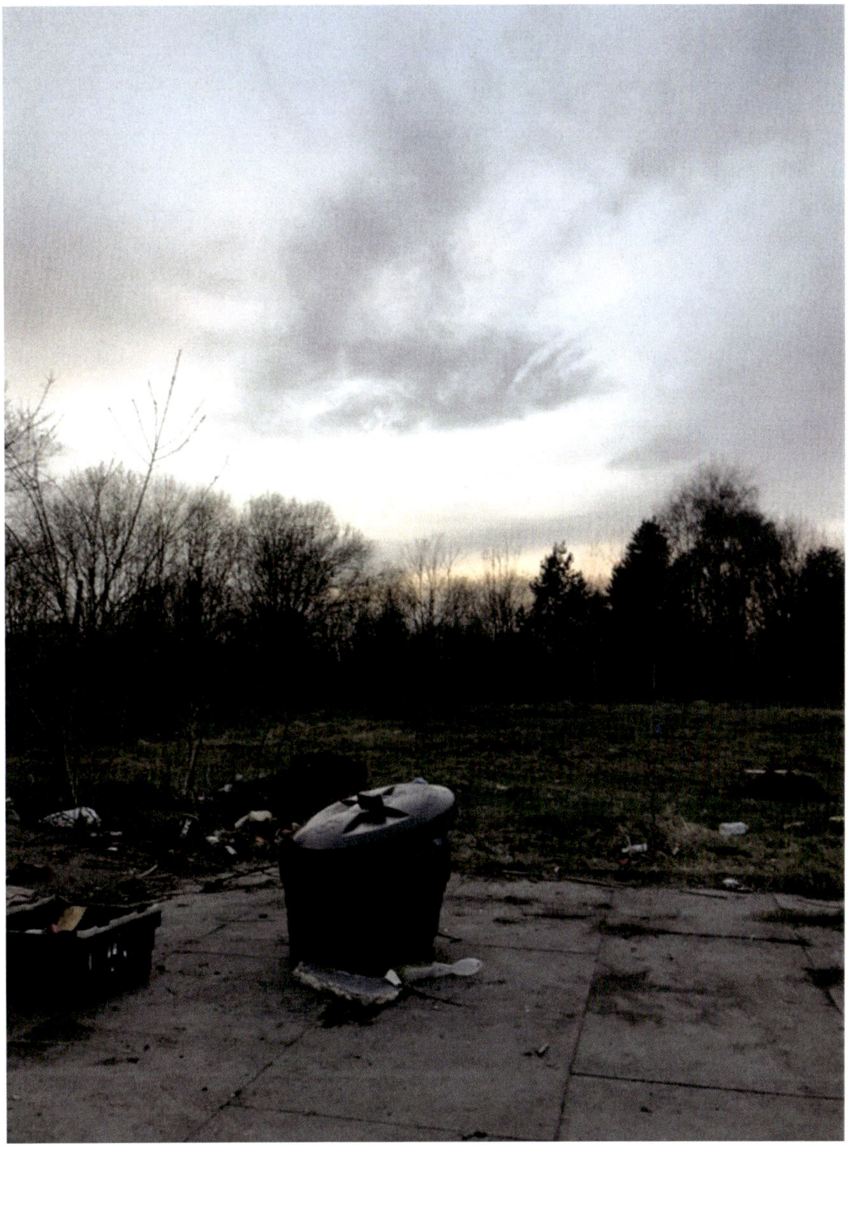

Posted by u/Satt**** 2 days ago

64

200 UGs **Crazyyyyy**

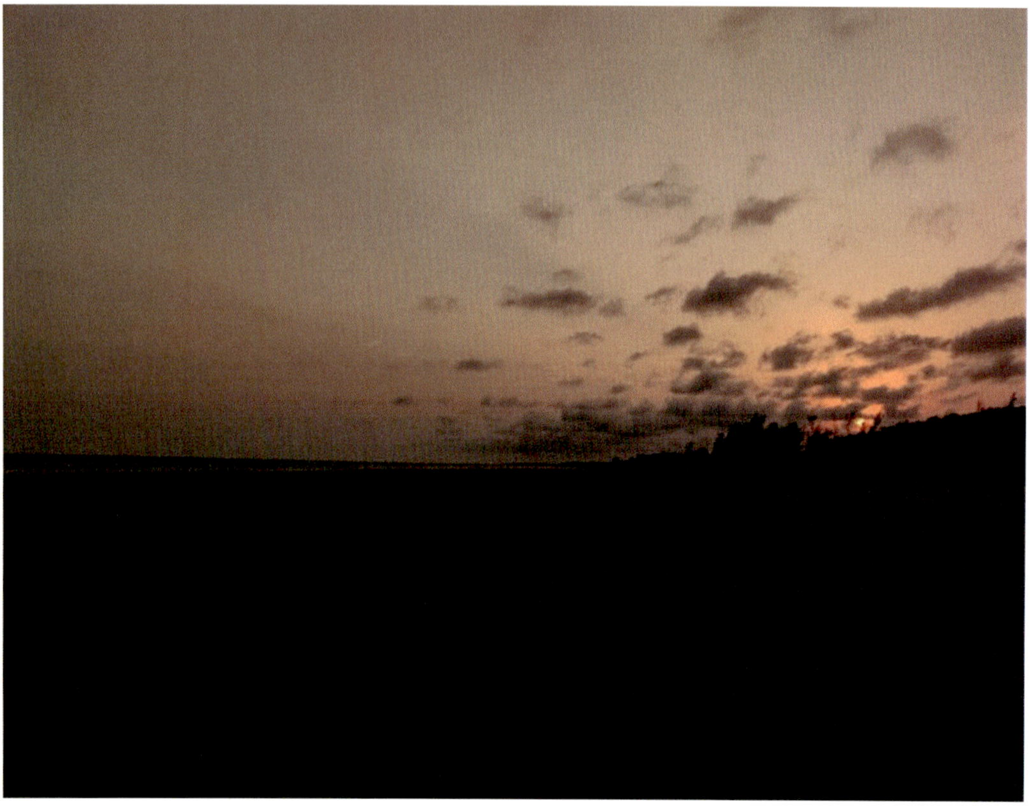

⬆ Posted by u/imno**** 2 days ago

79

⬇ **sugar looks nuts**

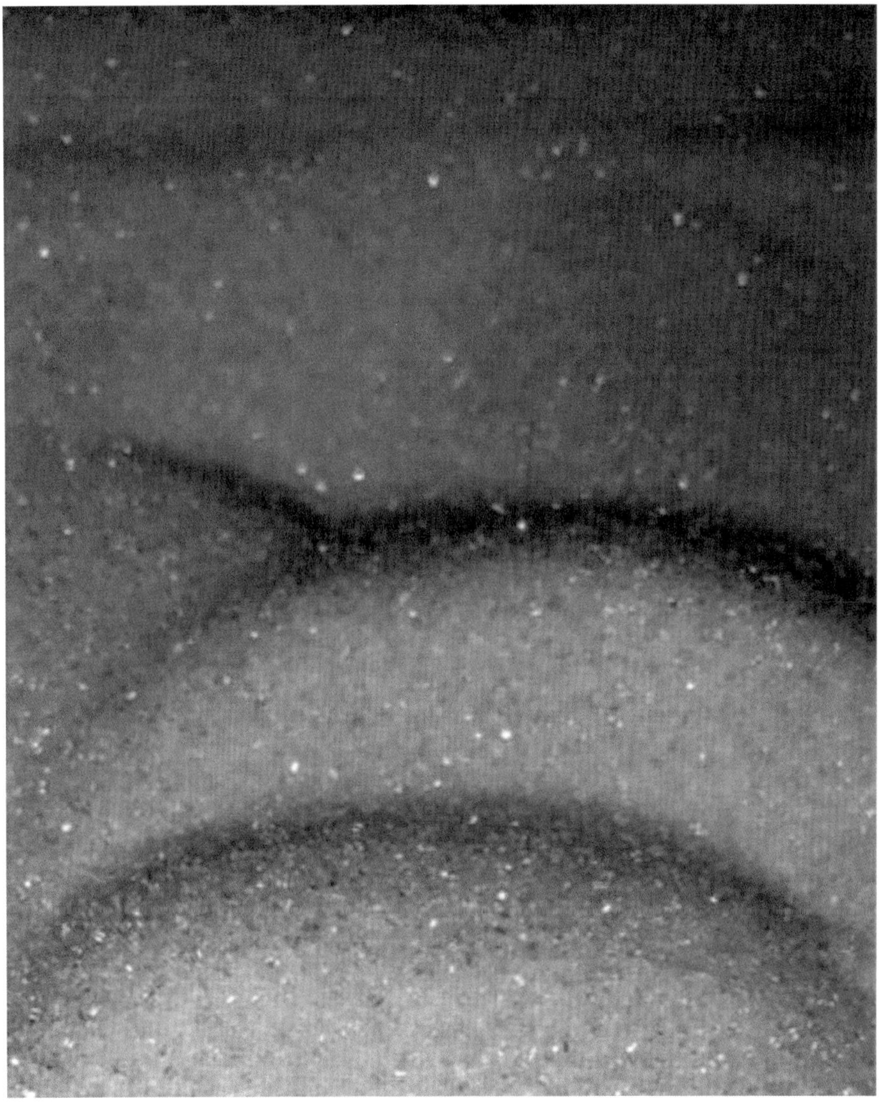

⬆ Posted by u/Kucf**** 5 days ago
22
⬇ 150 UGs **Nuts**

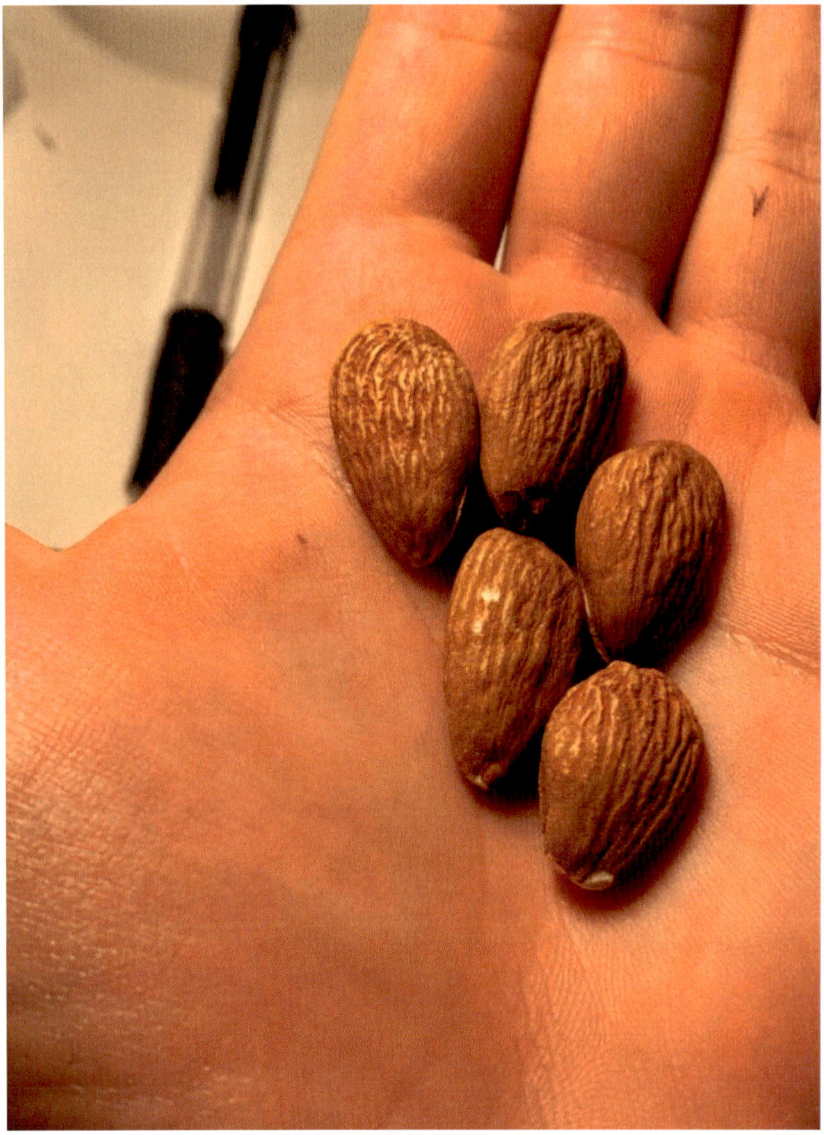

Posted by u/Abso**** 4 days ago

64

? Question ? **Holy shit**

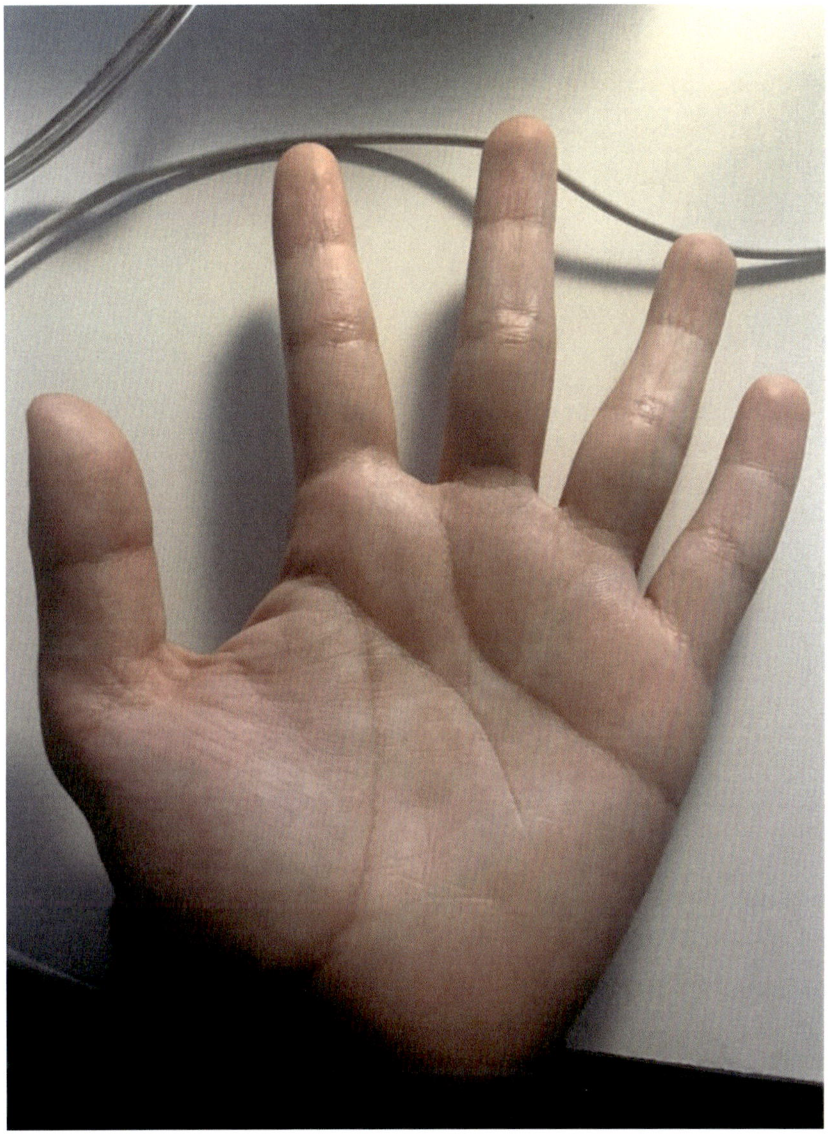

⬆ Posted by u/Dood**** 35 minutes ago
1
⬇ **Fuck, now i wanna trip and look at towels**

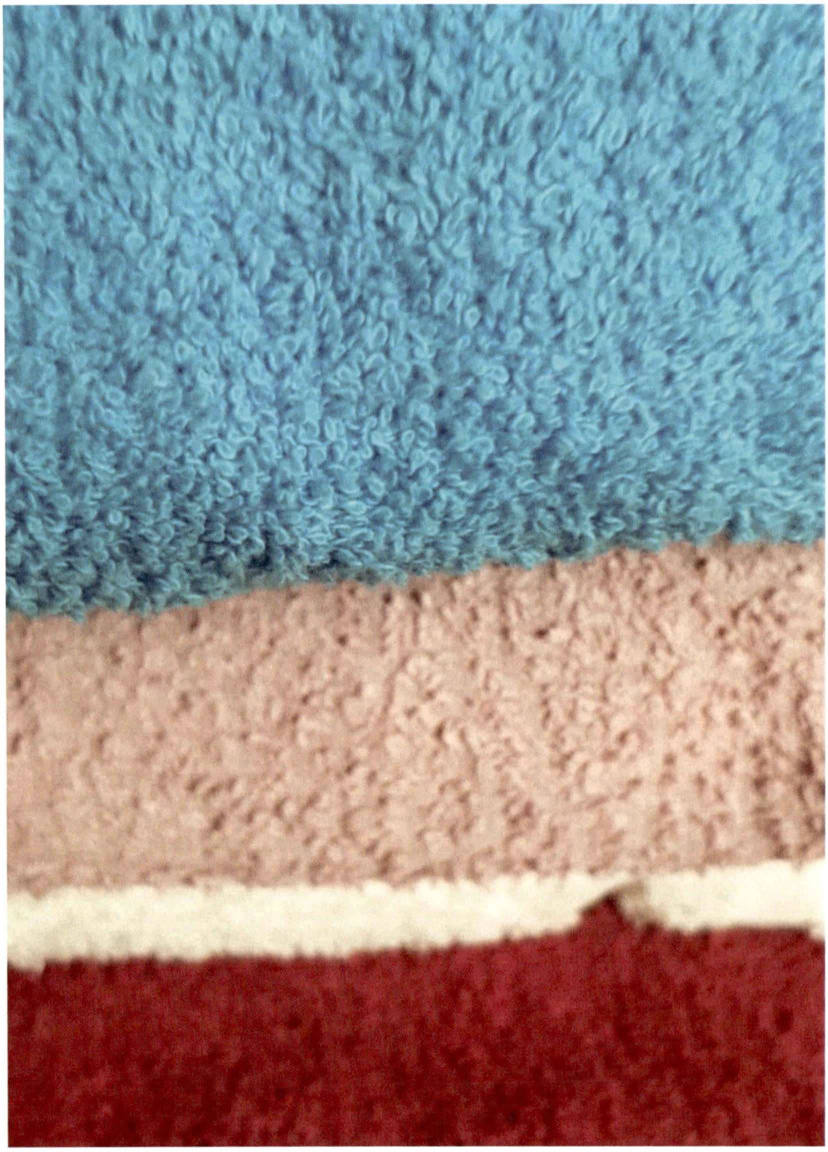

Posted by u/ASN3**** 2 days ago

10

Psychedelic Art

My bathroom mat tripped me the fuck out

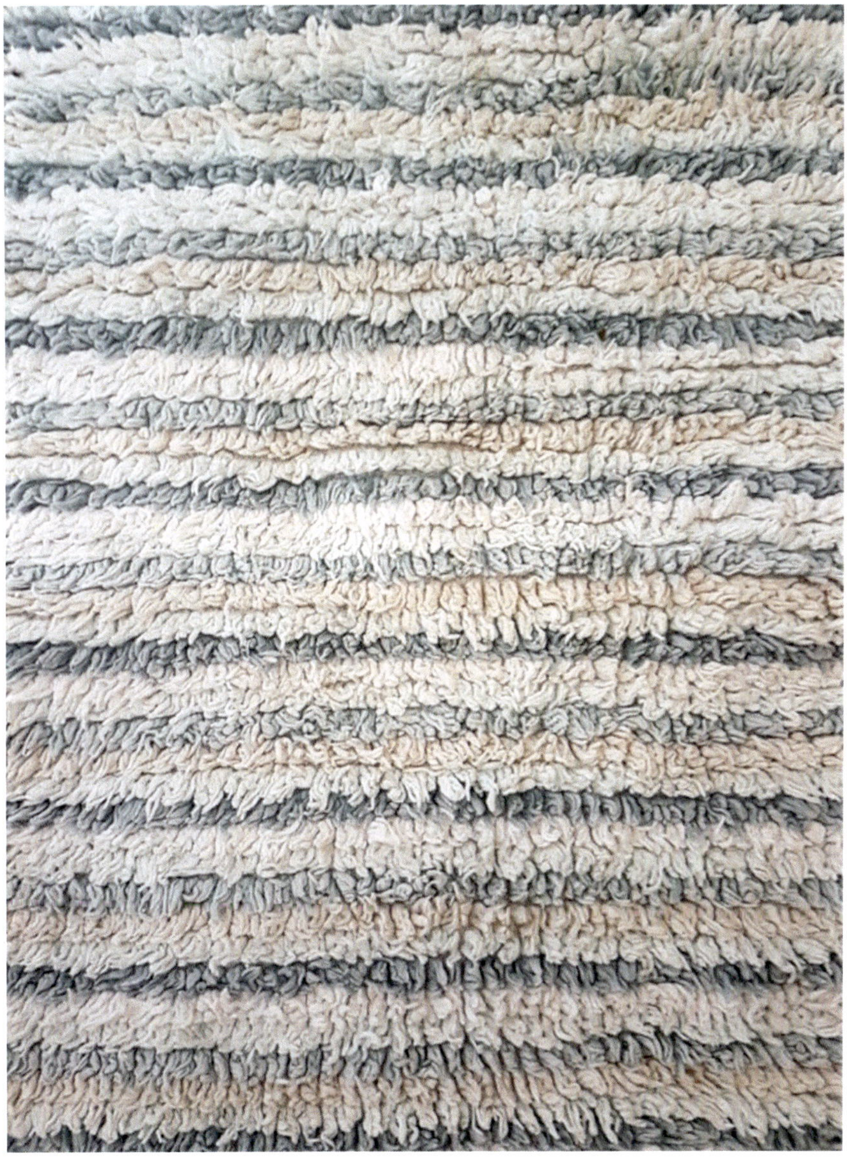

↑ Posted by u/Mada**** 1 day ago
45
↓
My new rug

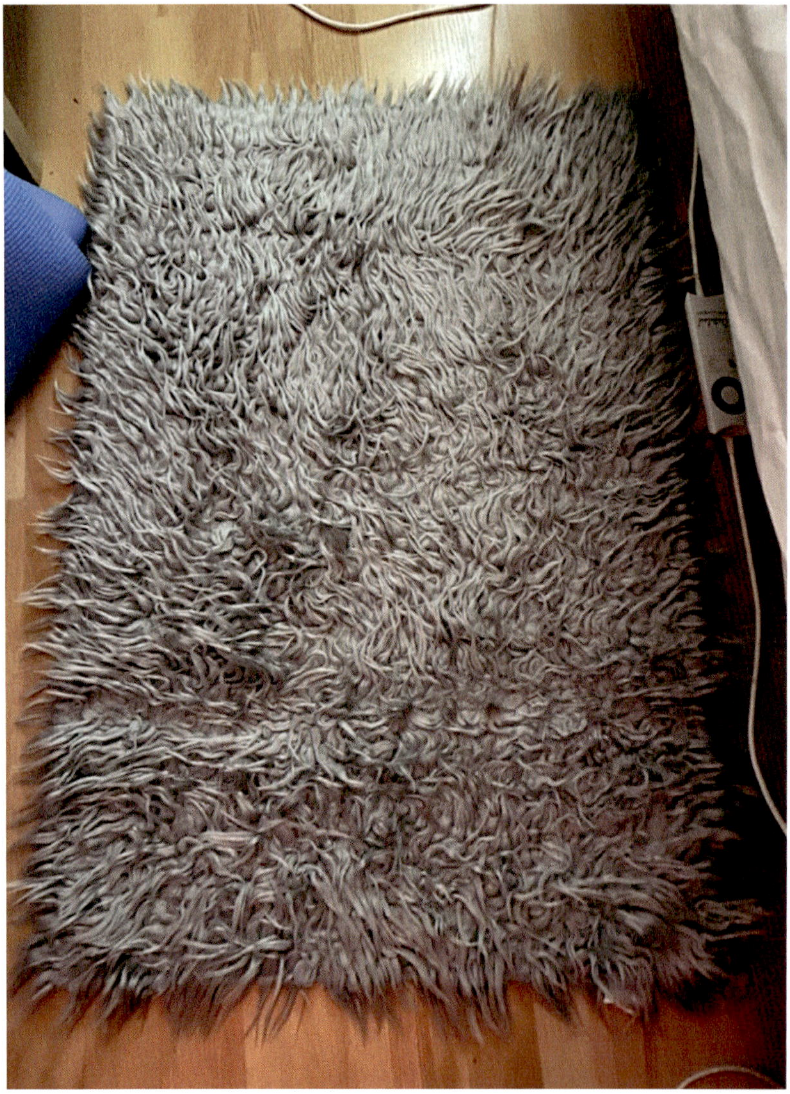

⬆ Posted by u/dyla**** 1 day ago

29

⬇ Currently Tripping **Holy shit**

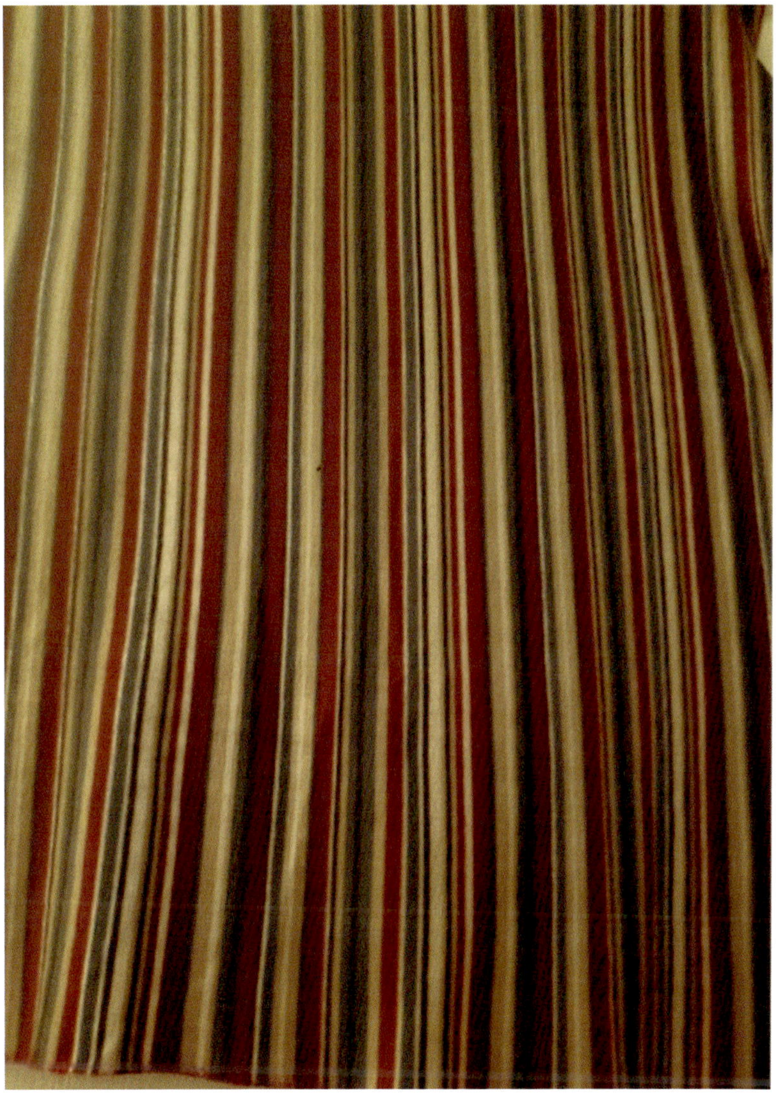

⬆ Posted by u/supe**** 2 days ago

39

⬇

Buuuuuut why?

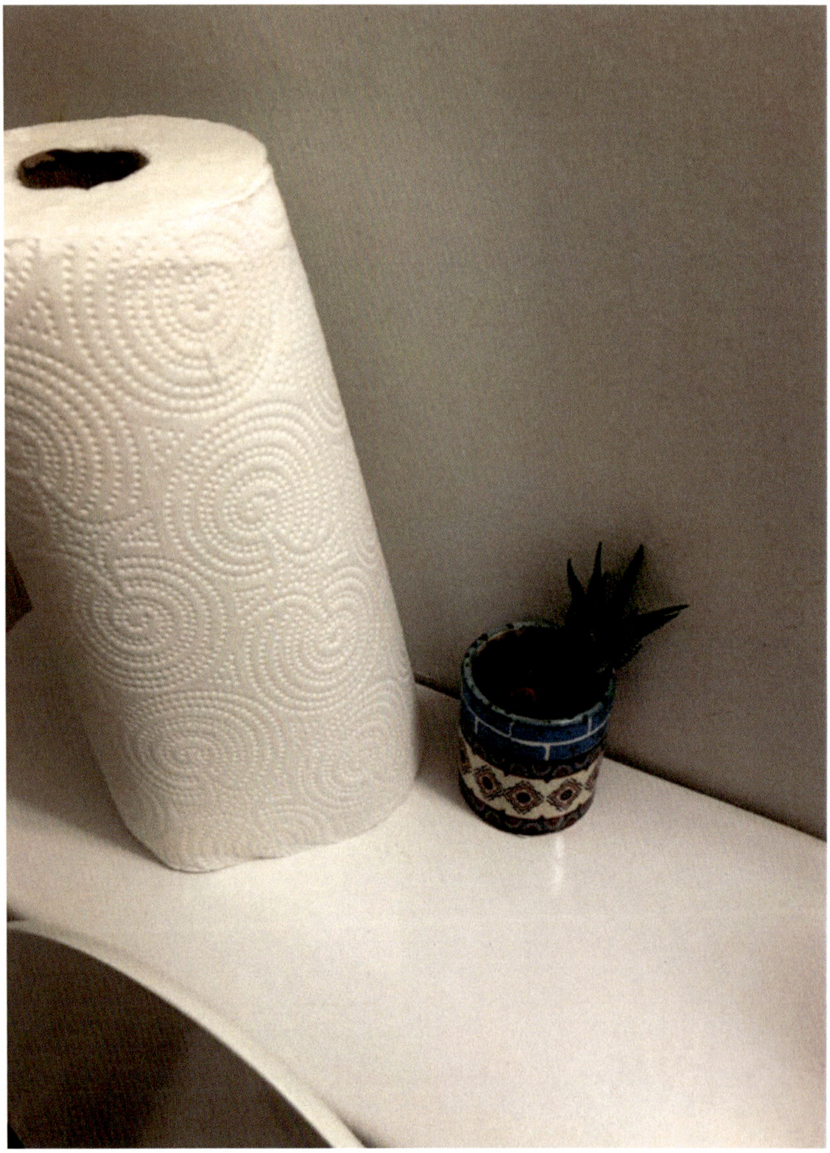

⬆ Posted by u/ambi**** 2 days ago
15
⬇ **stopped and stared at this**

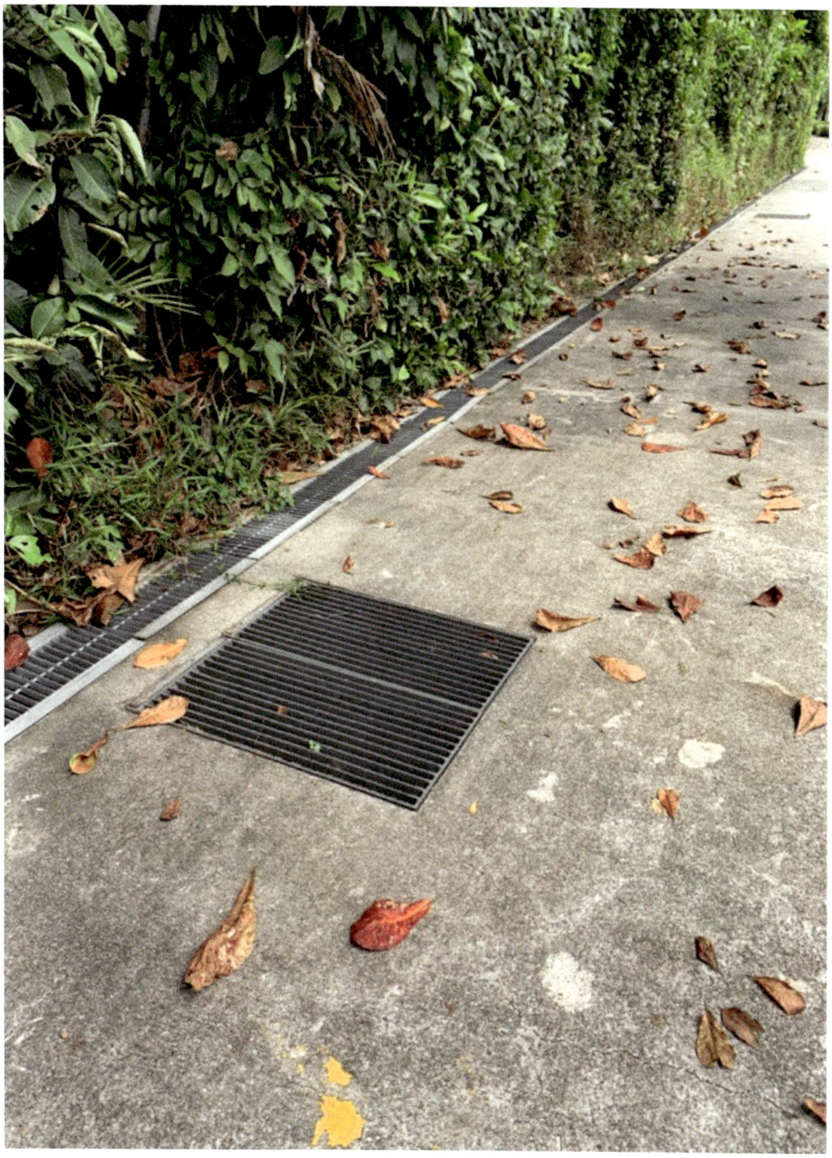

⬆ Posted by u/liam**** 2 days ago
28
⬇ Currently Tripping **hahahaha look at this**

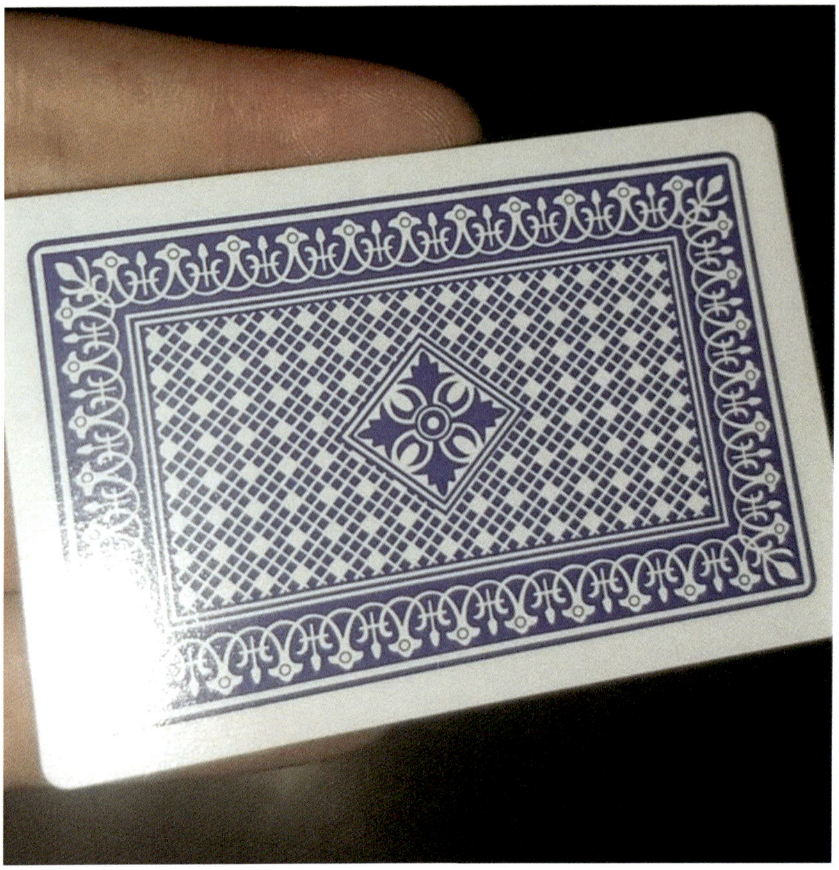

⬆ Posted by u/poop**** 1 day ago
10
⬇

✌ Currently Tripping ✌ **garfield is so pretty and handsome**

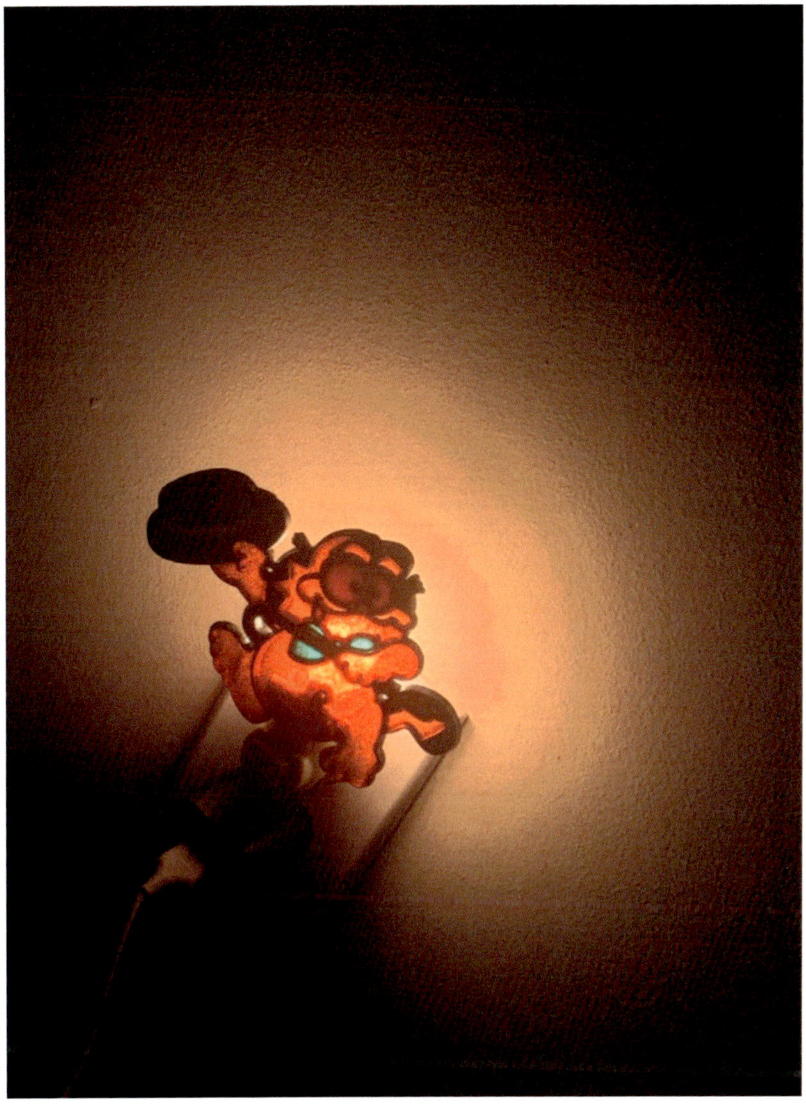

⬆ Posted by u/Beat**** 1 day ago
8
⬇ **Currently Tripping** **i see the meaning**

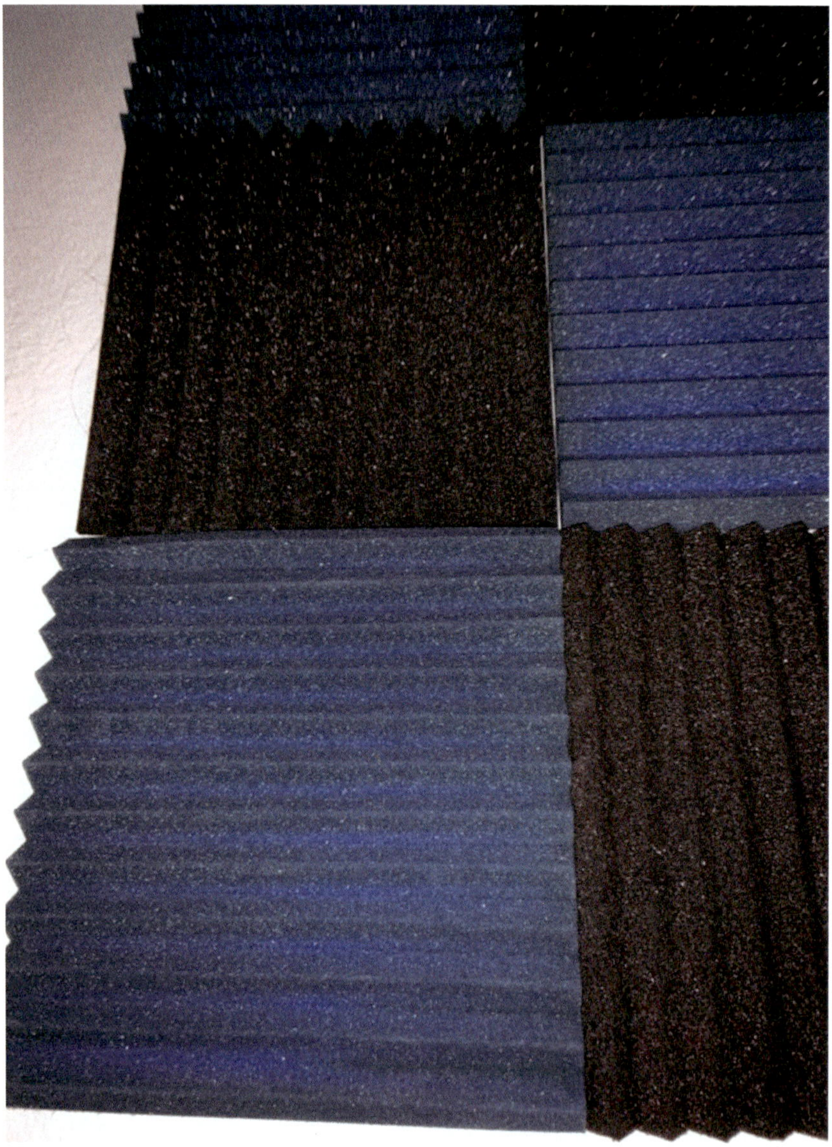

⬆ Posted by u/chod**** 1 day ago

20

⬇

A lot to take in

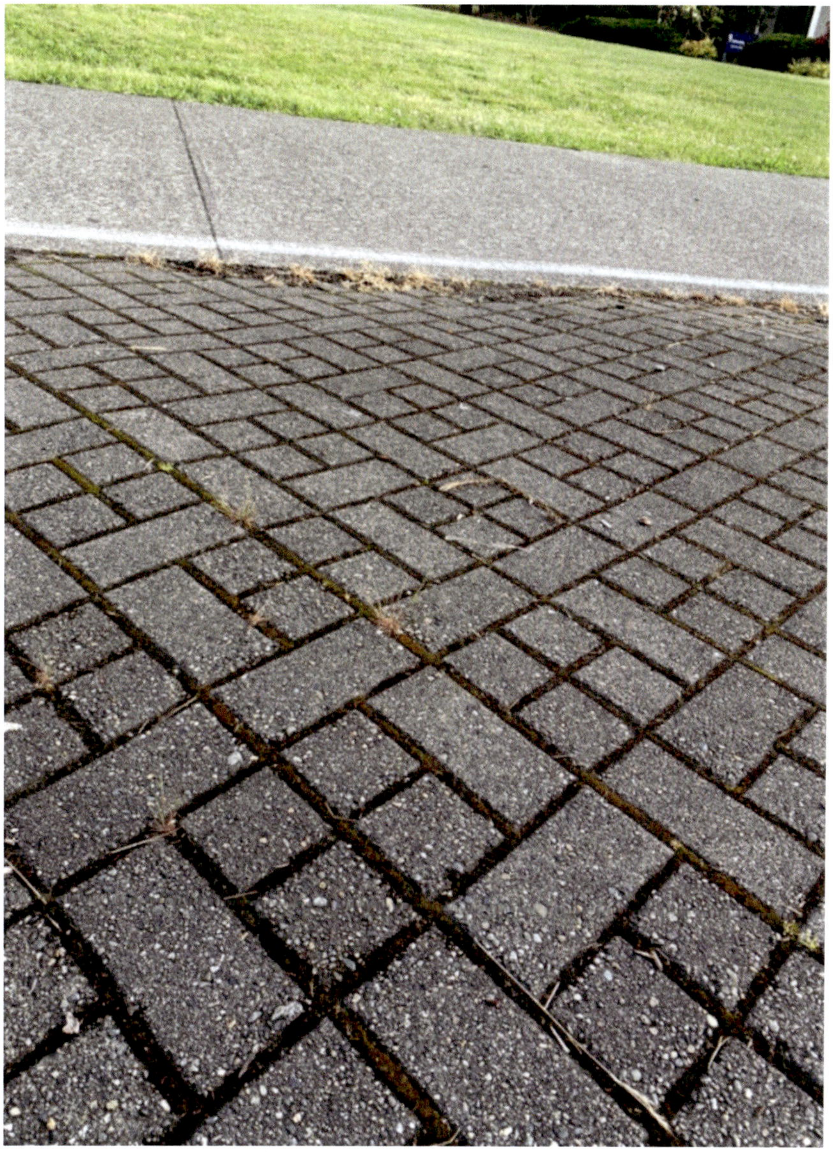

⬆ Posted by u/Roxa**** 1 day ago
83
⬇ **Psychedelic Art** **The ridges in my dogs nose tho**

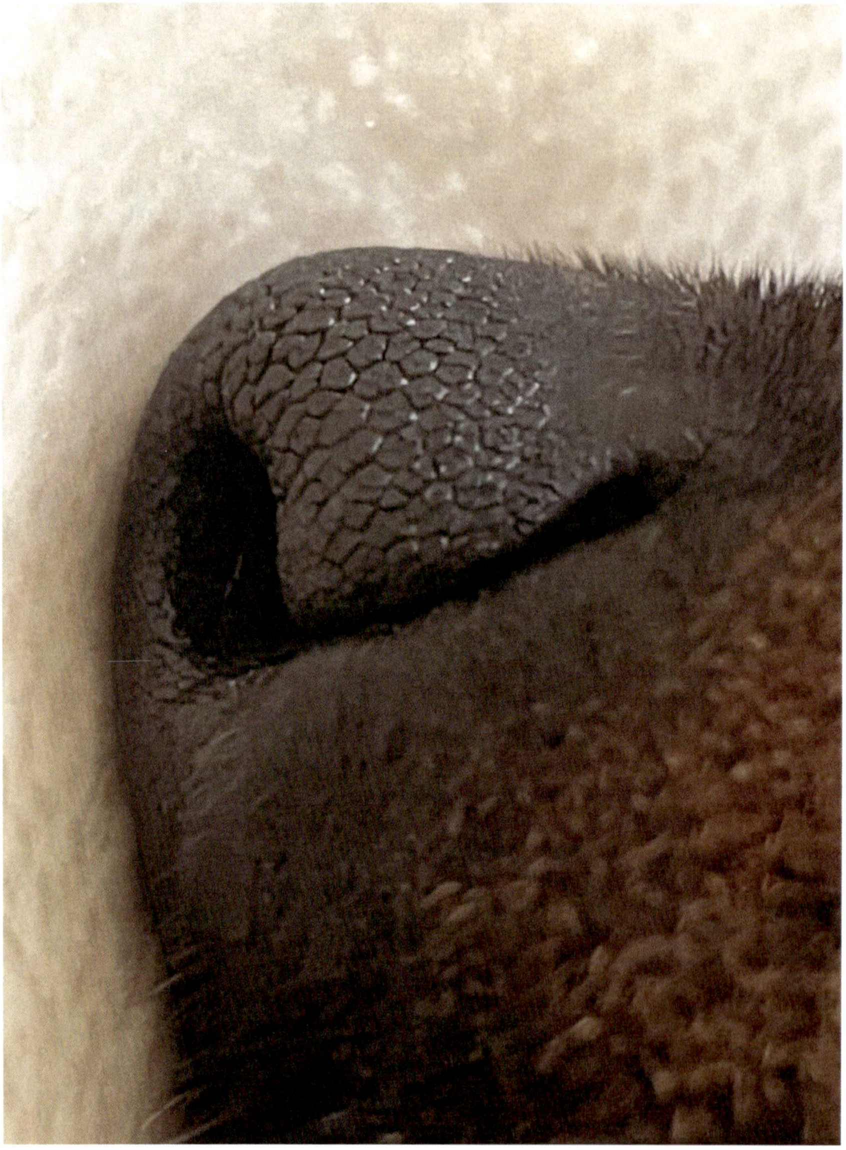

⬆ Posted by u/yung**** 4 days ago
114
⬇ ✌ Currently Tripping ✌ **Woah**

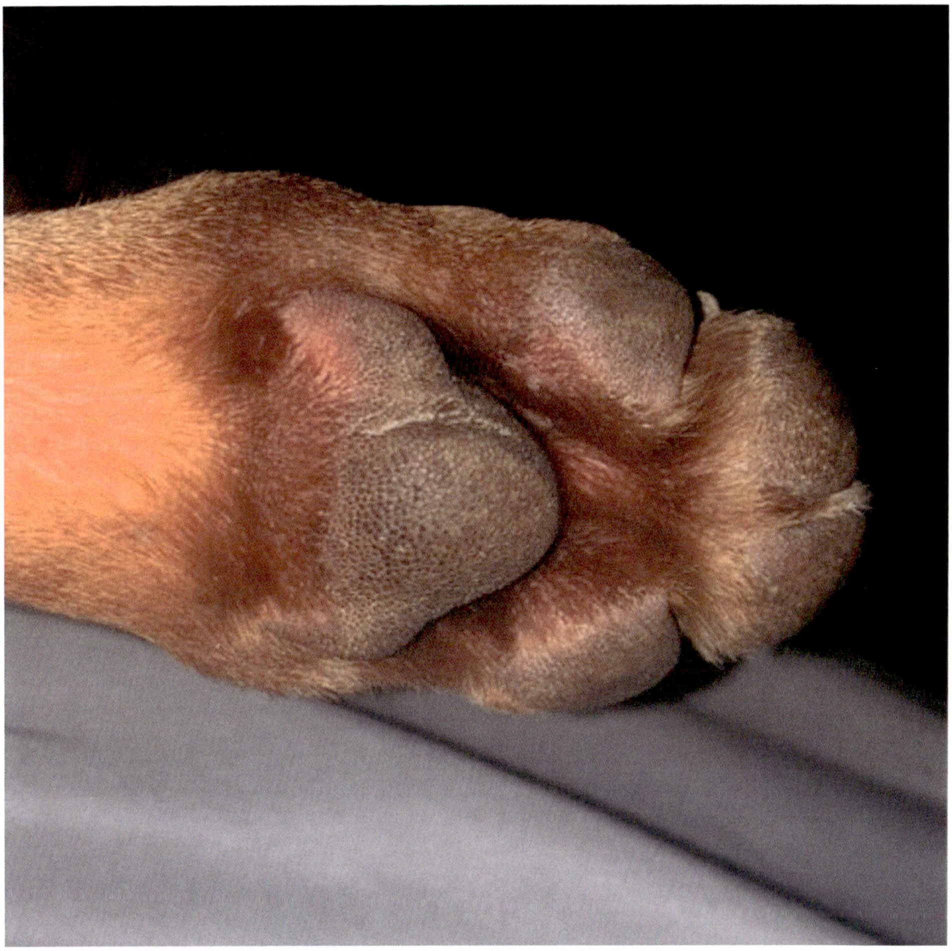

Posted by u/Suck**** 1 day ago

276

Bruh... The ceiling of my apartment

Posted by u/Hock**** 4 days ago

43

100 UGs **The ceilings tell stories I swear**

Posted by u/shee**** 2 days ago

415

250 UGs Ceiling rose in my house

Posted by u/ragi**** 2 days ago

39

Currently Tripping **Woah**

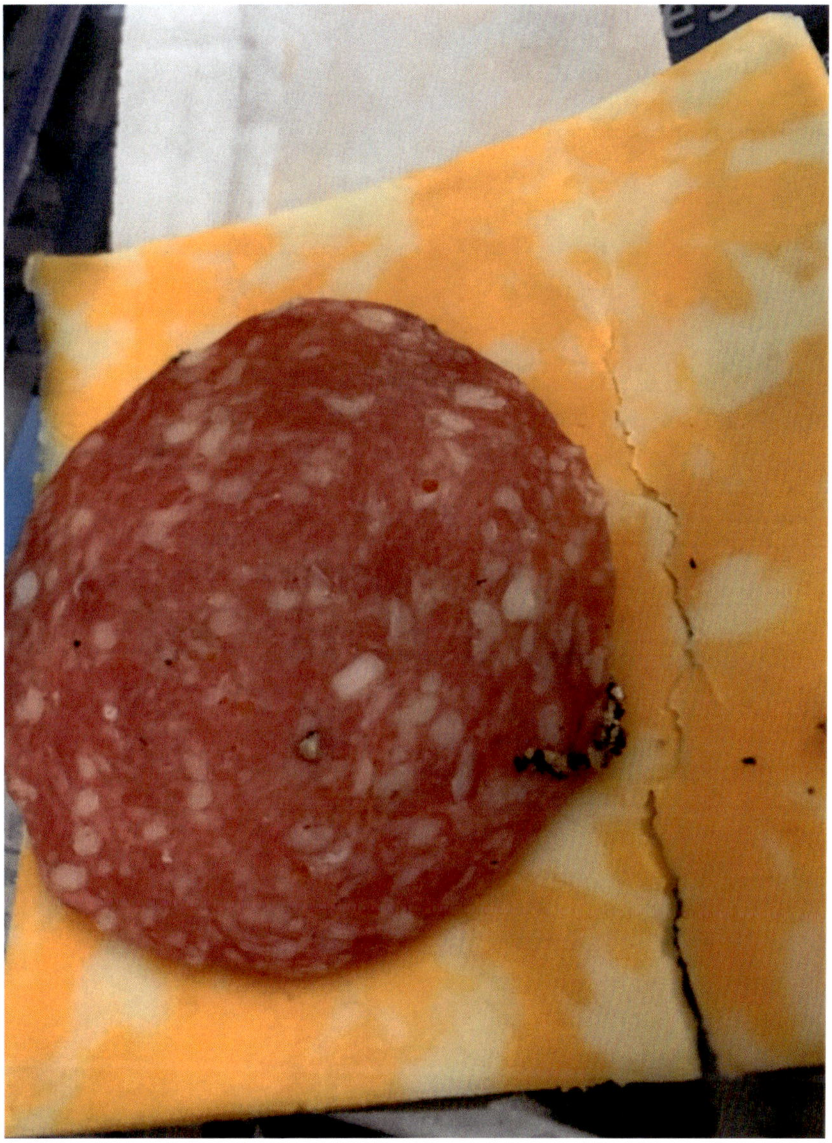

↑ Posted by u/Aece**** 1 day ago
14
↓

Pepper skin is so mesmerizing

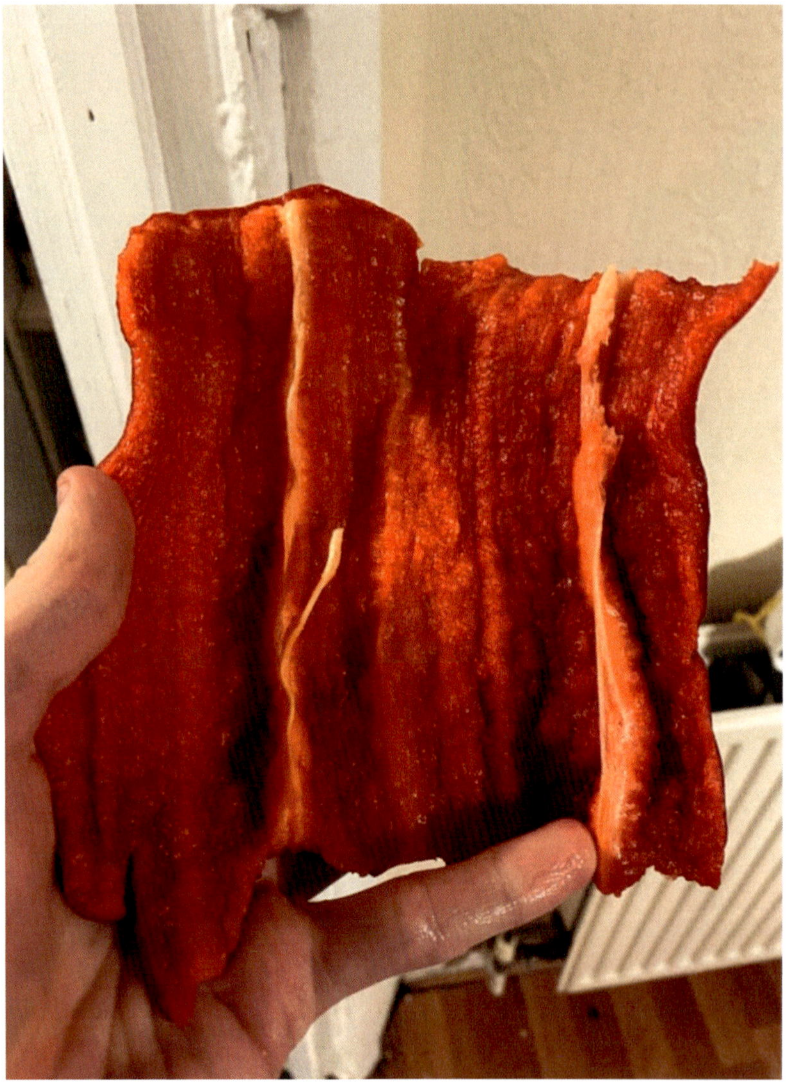

⬆ Posted by u/Meel**** 5 days ago

320

⬇ ✌ Currently Tripping ✌ **Wow**

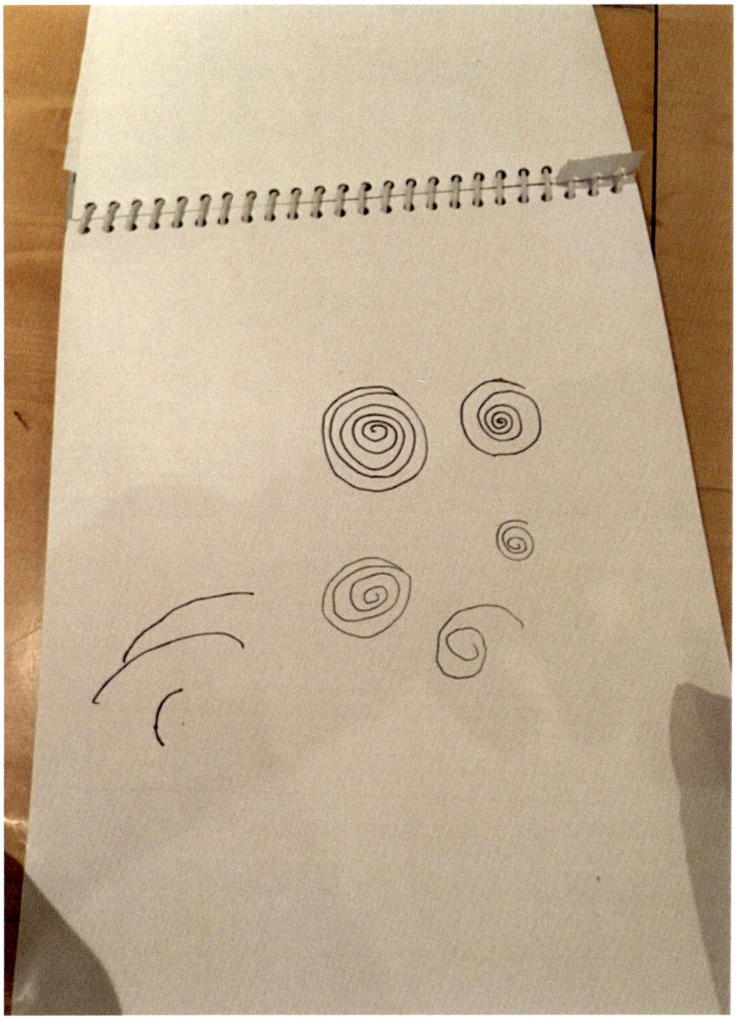

Posted by u/Offi**** 20 hours ago

0

Currently Tripping **Cool**

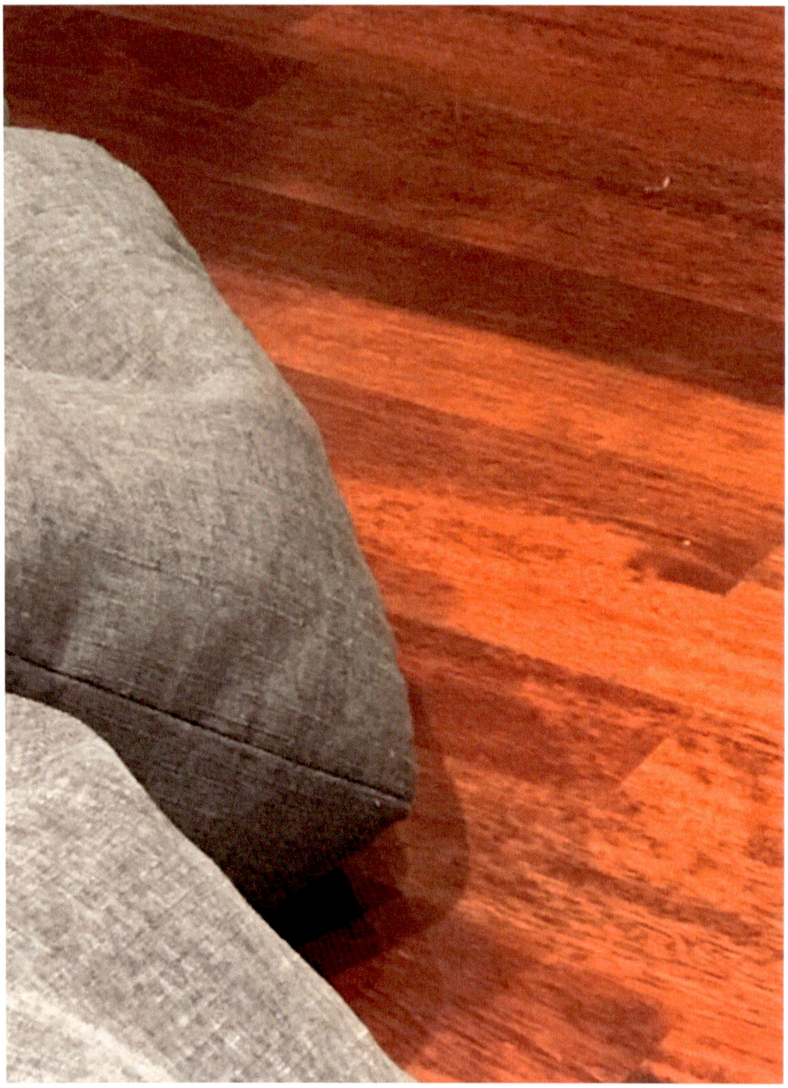

↑ Posted by u/twin**** 5 days ago

126

↓

GAWD DMANN

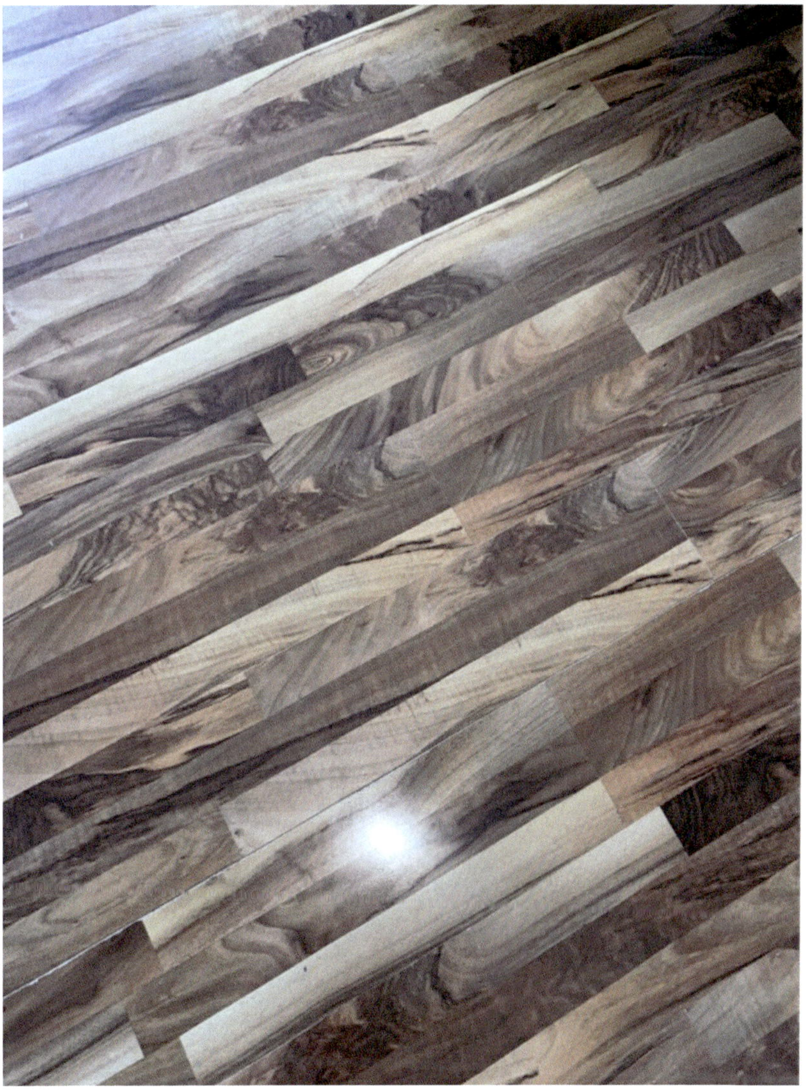

⬆ Posted by u/JoTh**** 1 day ago
159
⬇ Currently Tripping **HOLY FUCKING SHIT**

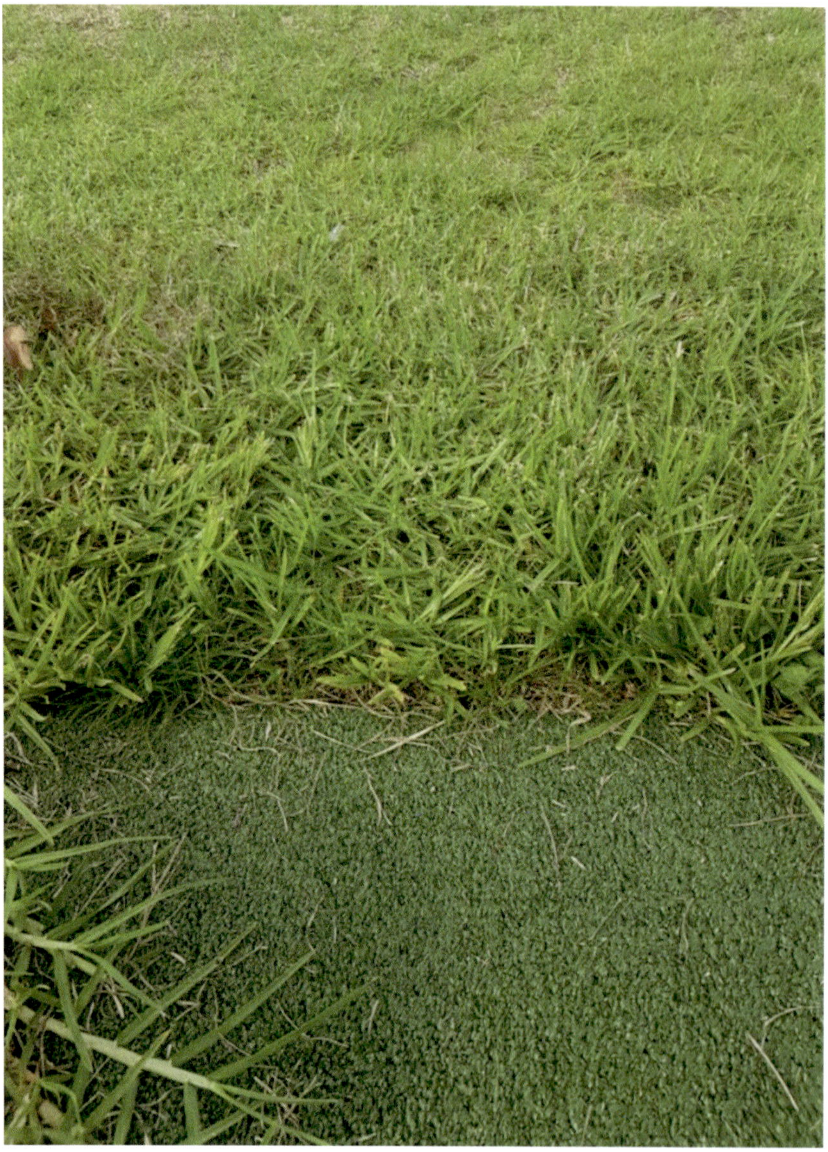

↑ Posted by u/wers**** 3 hours ago
6
↓ Nature trip **Little buddy**

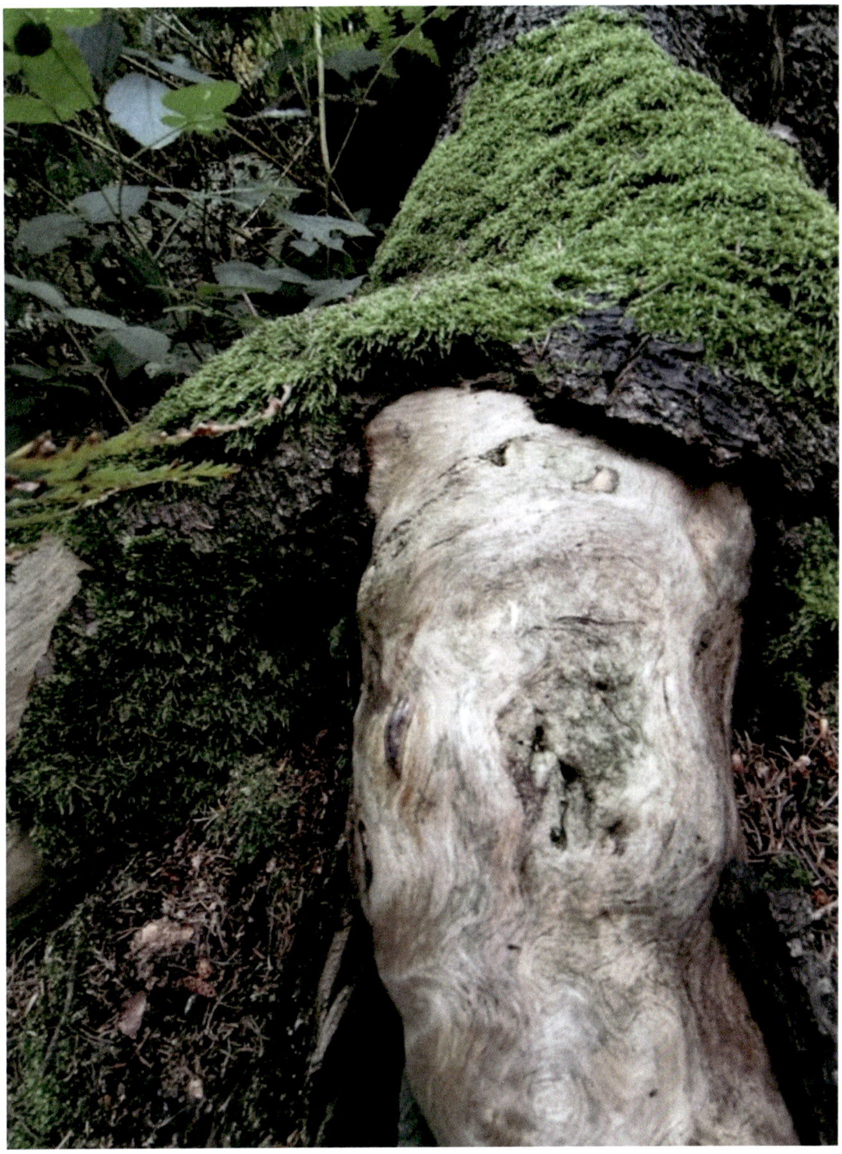

⬆ Posted by u/dari**** 9 hours ago
38
⬇

✌ **Currently Tripping** ✌ **Holy shit**

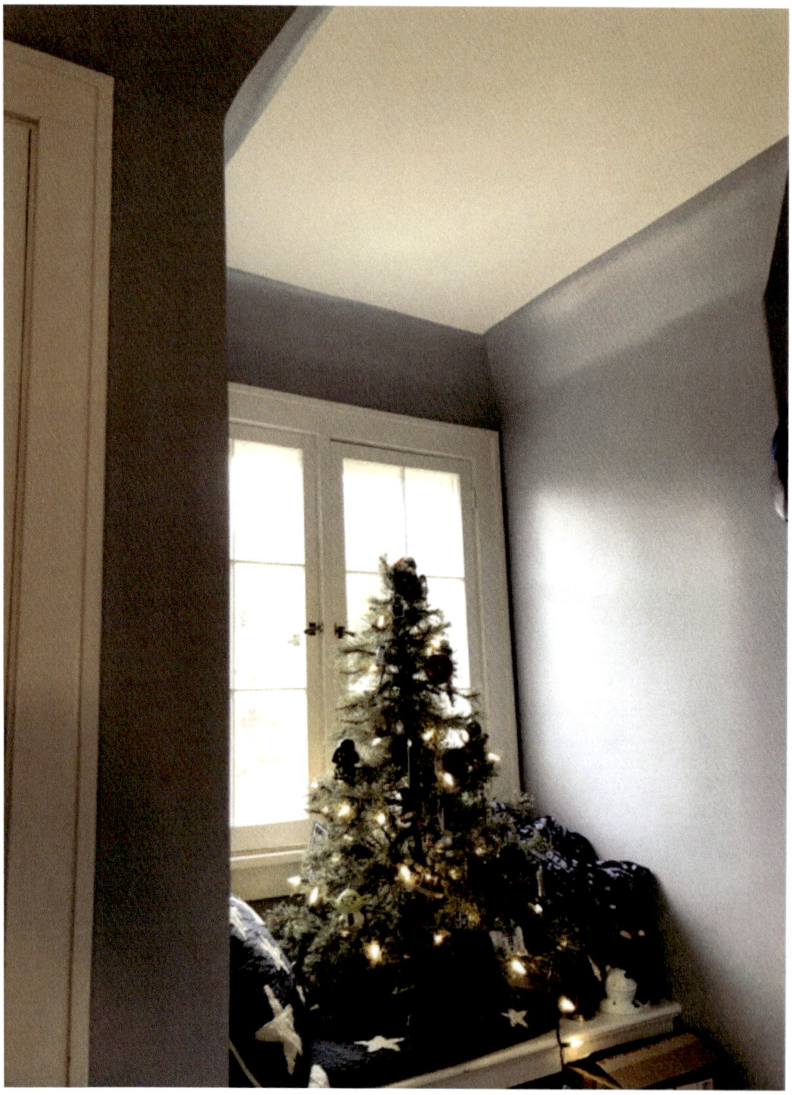

⬆ Posted by u/chris**** 4 days ago
85
⬇ ✌Currently Tripping✌ **Astounding**

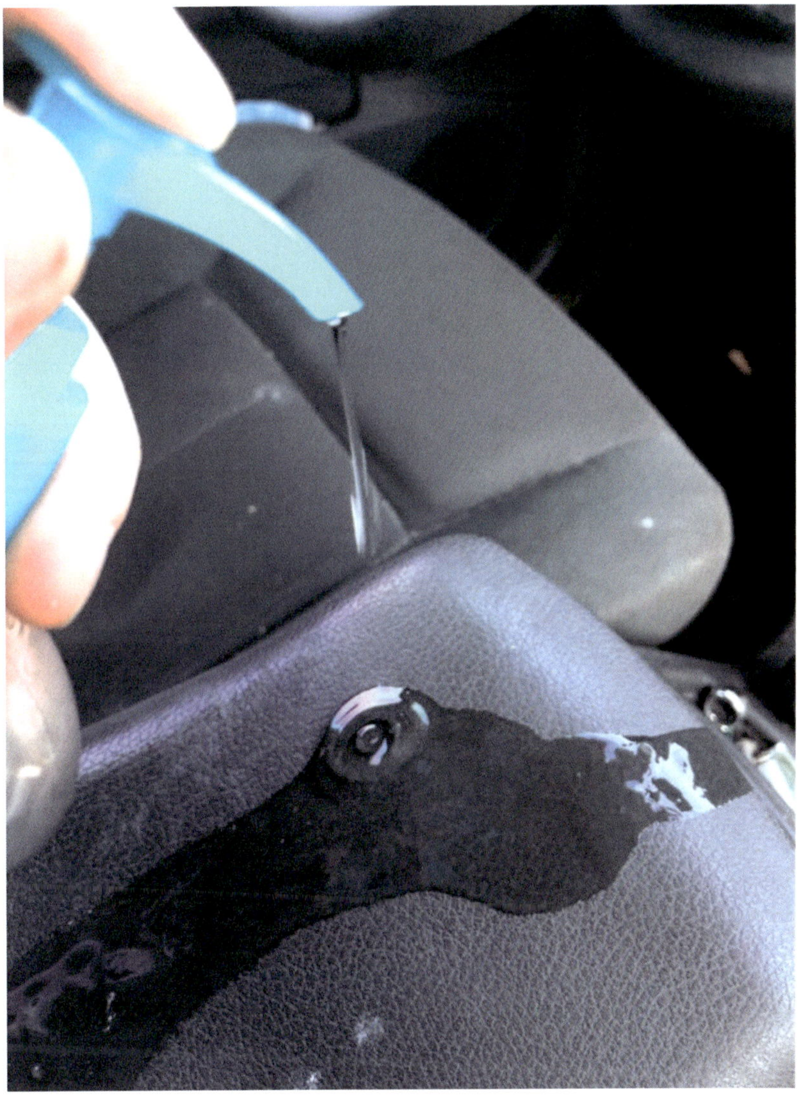

Posted by u/chas**** 2 days ago

38

✌ Currently Tripping ✌ **always be ending up here**

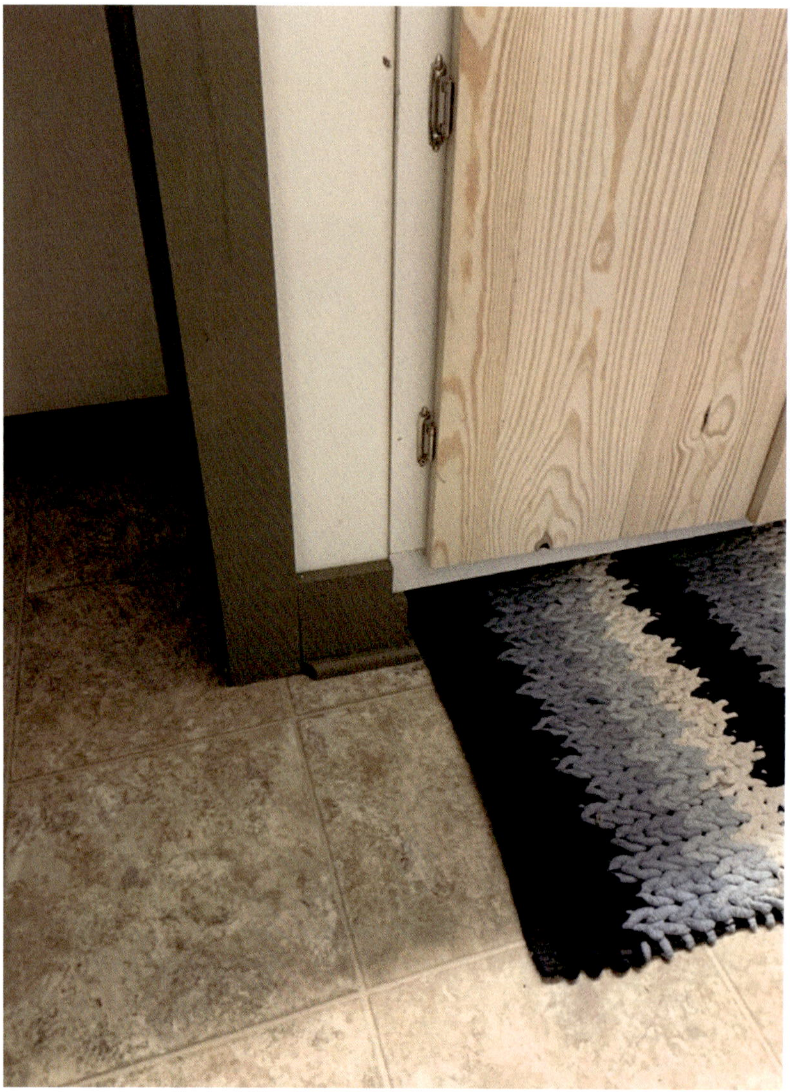

Posted by u/1425**** 4 days ago

114

✌ Currently Tripping ✌

I always get stuck in this bathroom

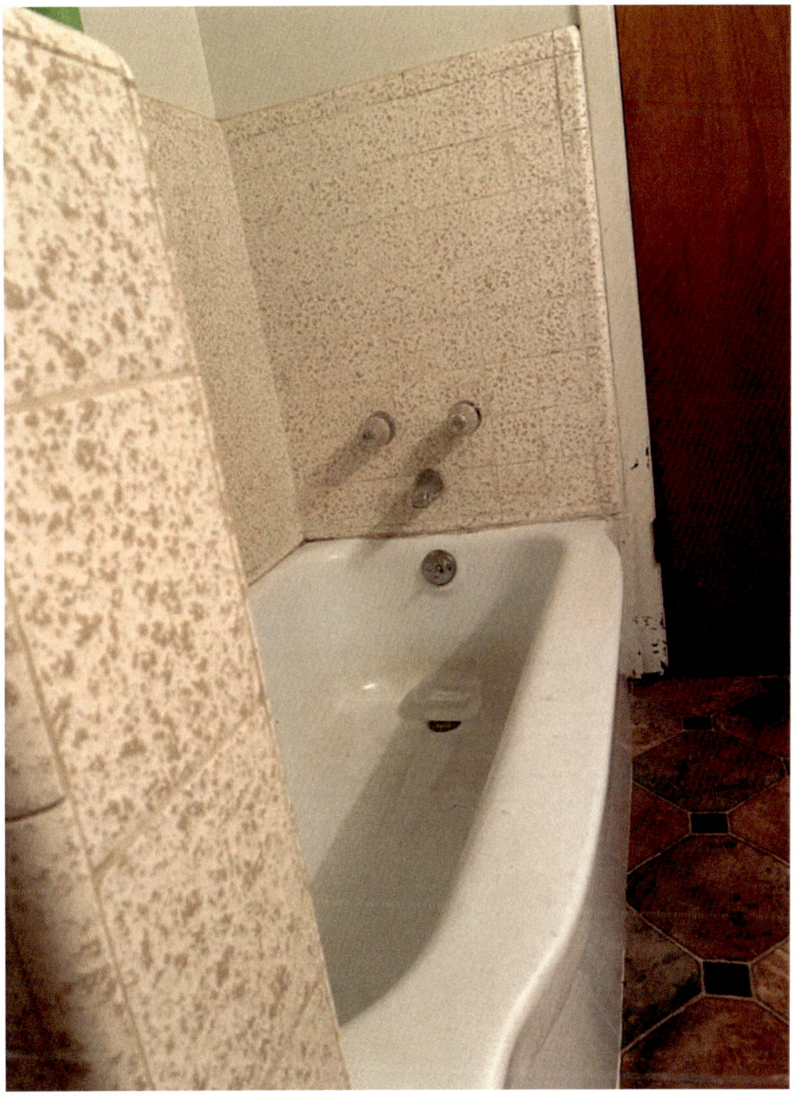

⬆ Posted by u/ANDR**** 1 day ago

3

⬇ **Woah.**

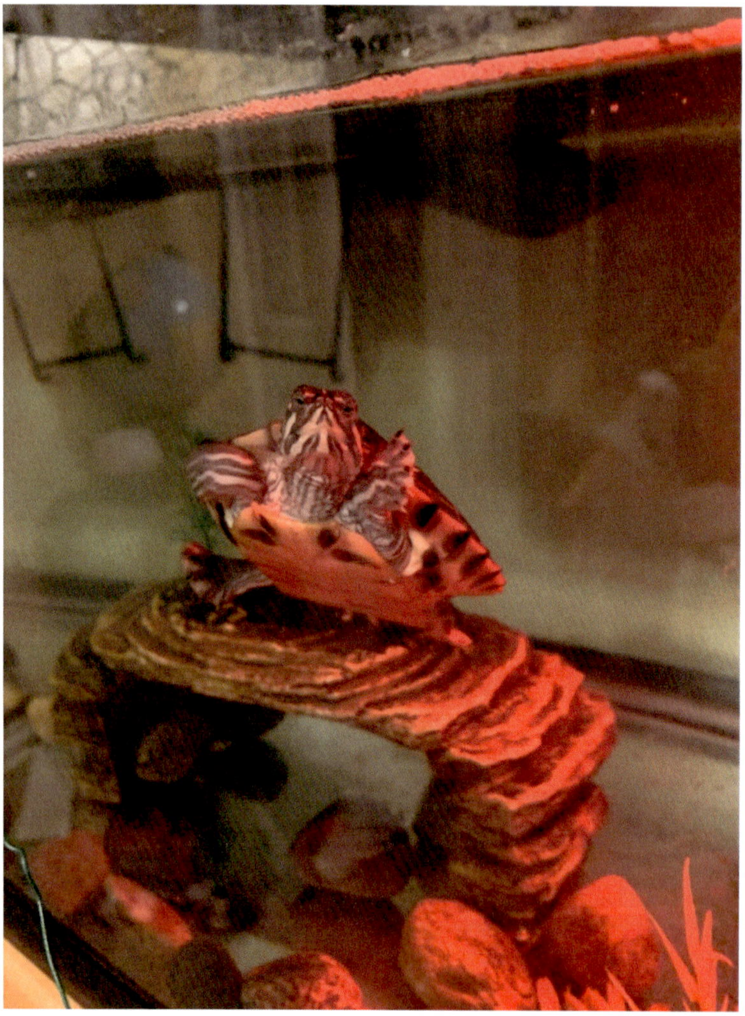

Posted by u/Lapi**** 1 day ago

25

Challenging Trip

5 hours in and that lump of hummus has formed into a frog

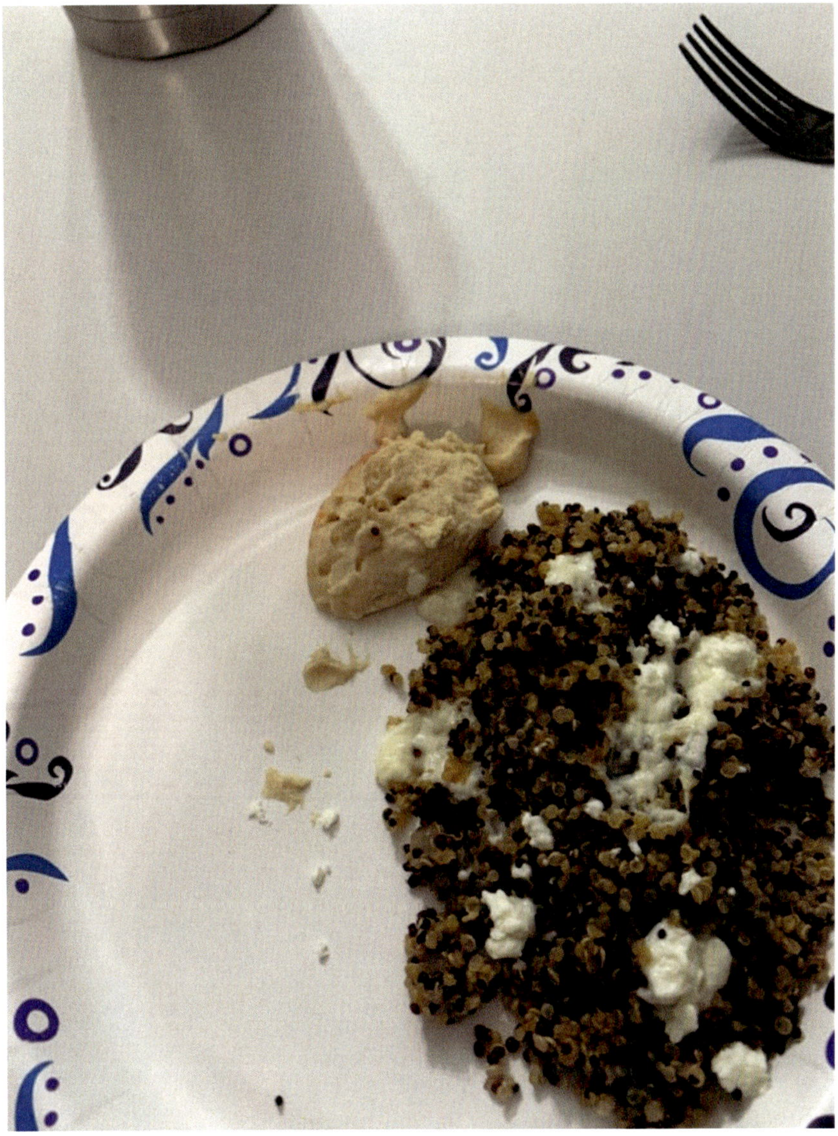

⬆ Posted by u/lmno**** 1 day ago
34
⬇ Group trip **Post trip world is lovely**

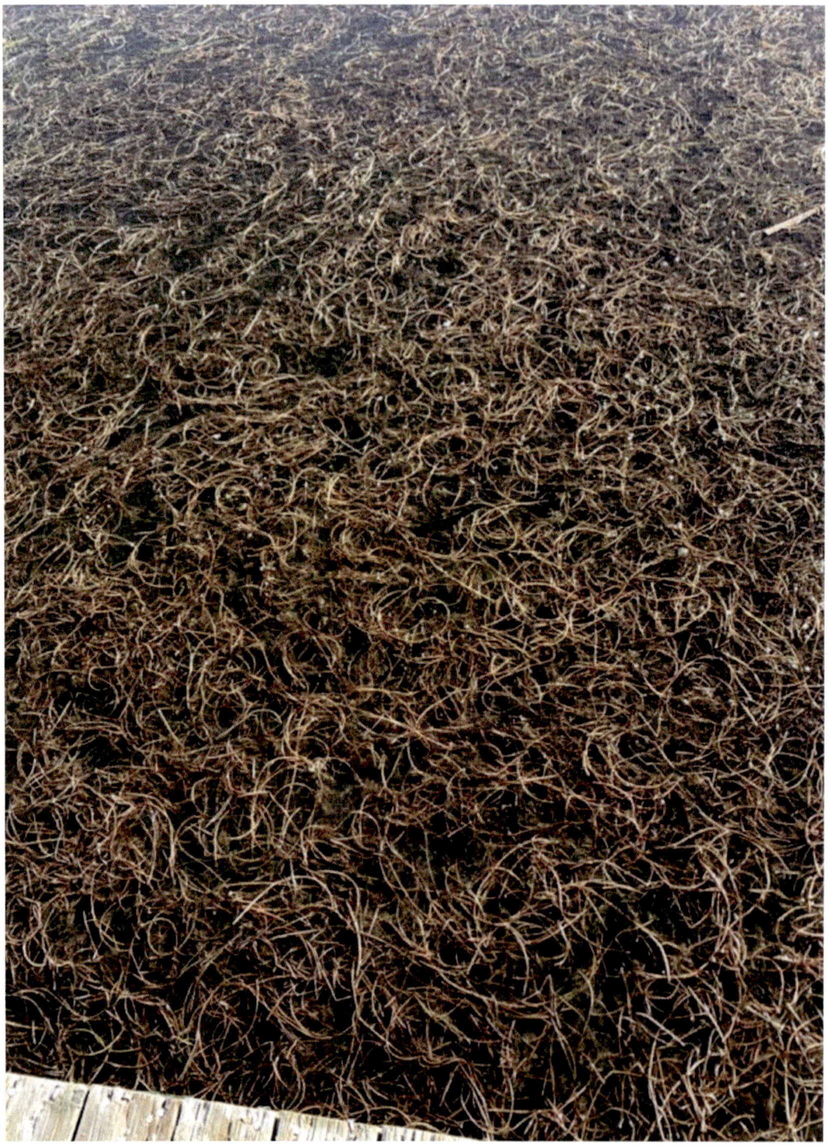

⬆ Posted by u/poop**** 4 days ago
4
⬇ **What the fu k**

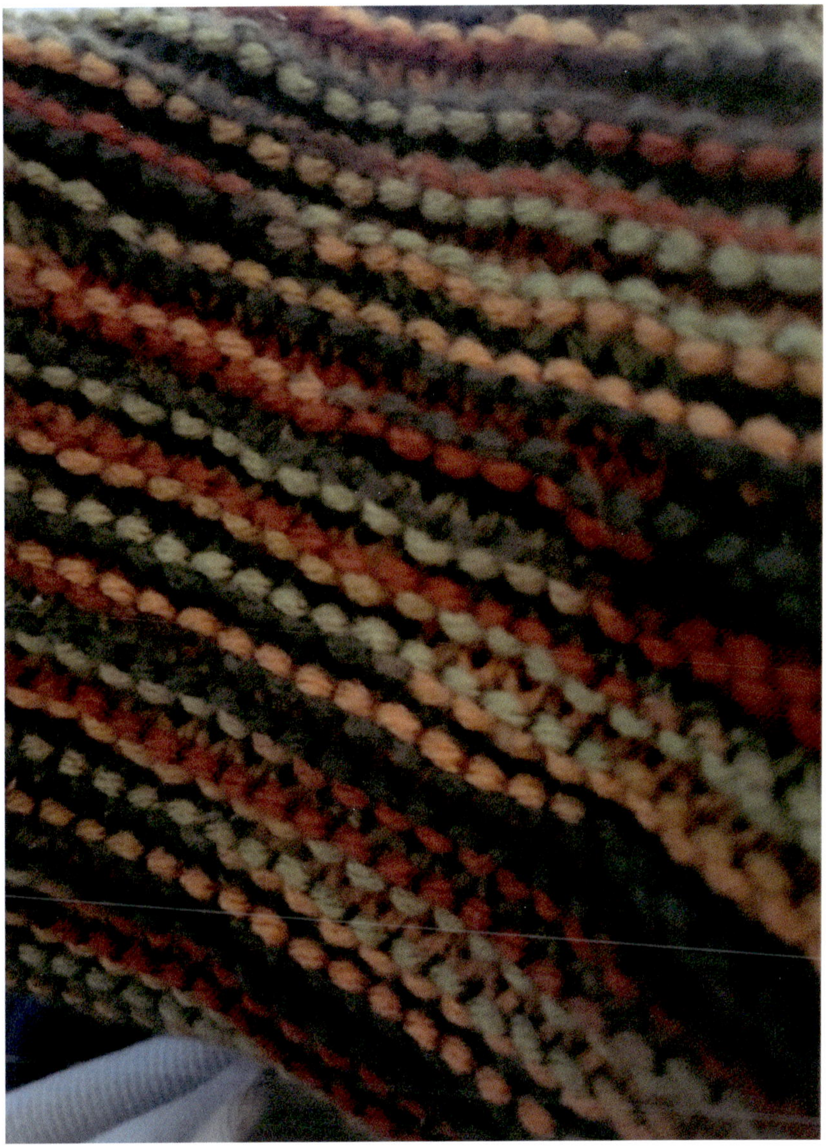

Posted by u/irea**** 2 days ago

20

First trip **bruh**

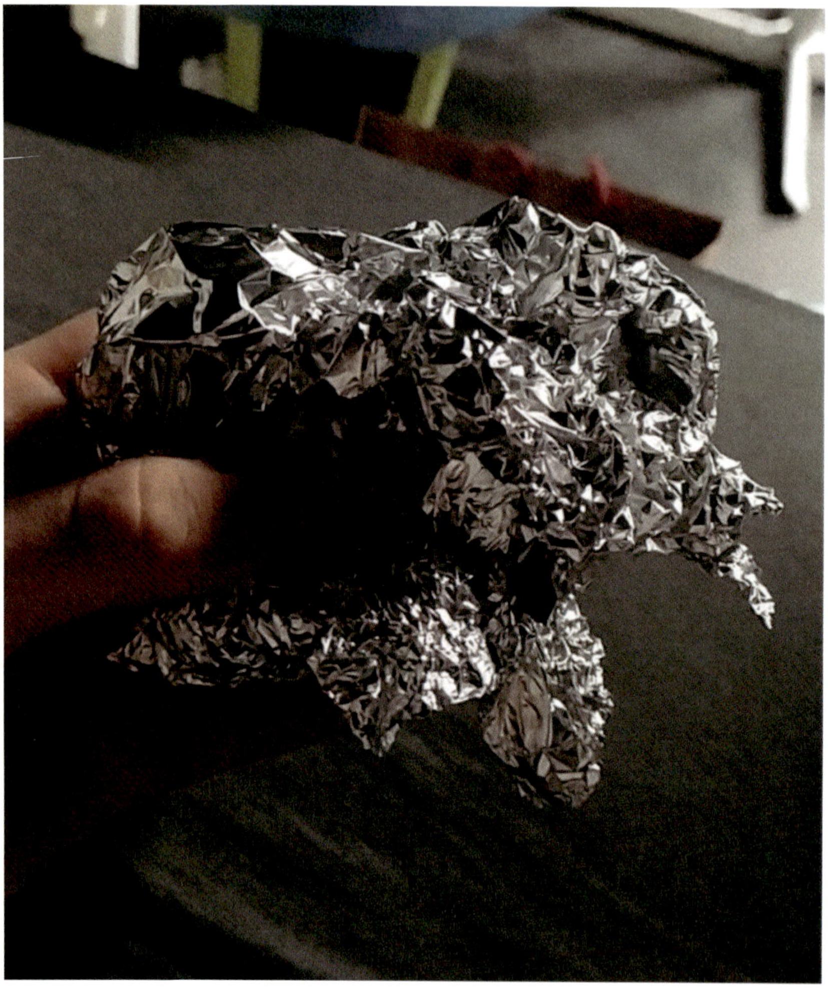

Posted by u/fgoo**** 3 days ago

7

150 UGs

Full moon and crazy fast moving clouds...

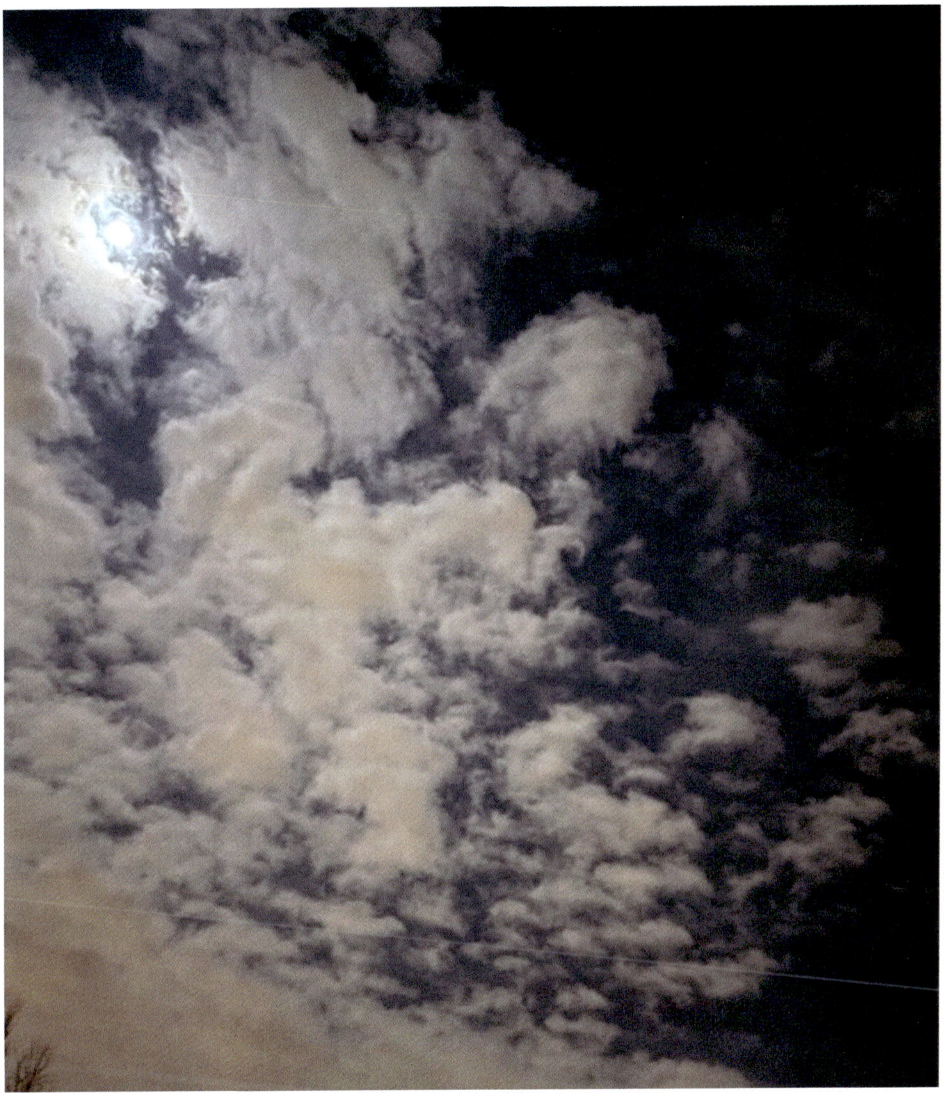

Posted by u/rott**** 1 day ago

2

cool shit **miso soup separation**

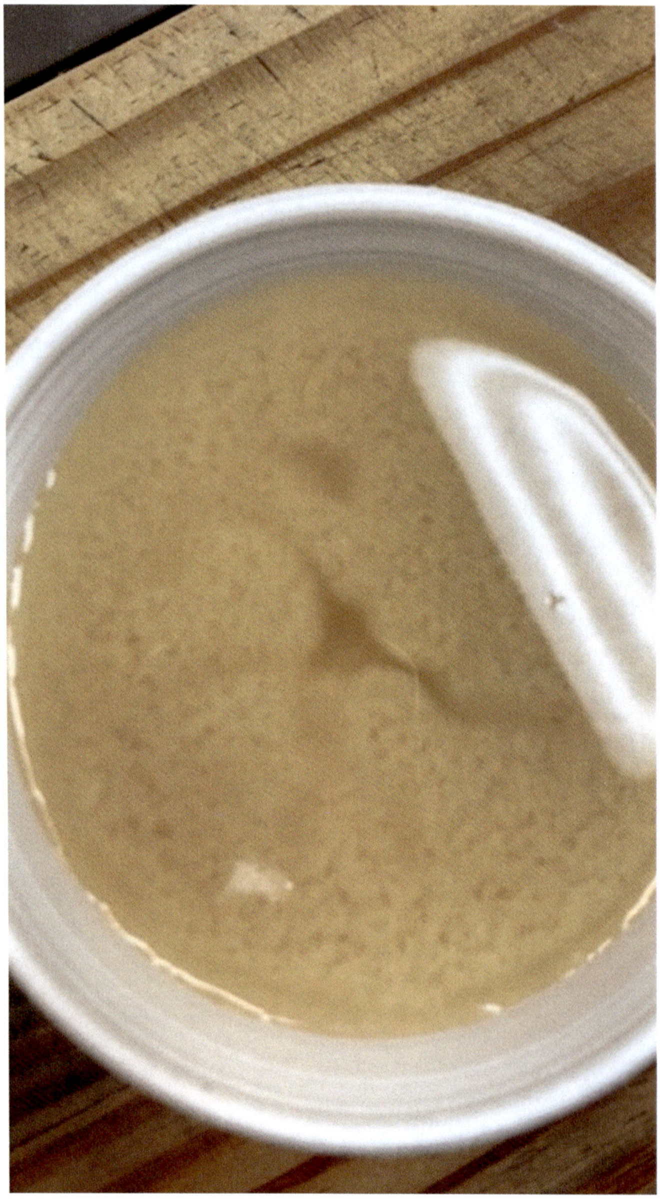

⬆ Posted by u/mufr**** 15 hours ago

39

⬇

I found the fucking yeti

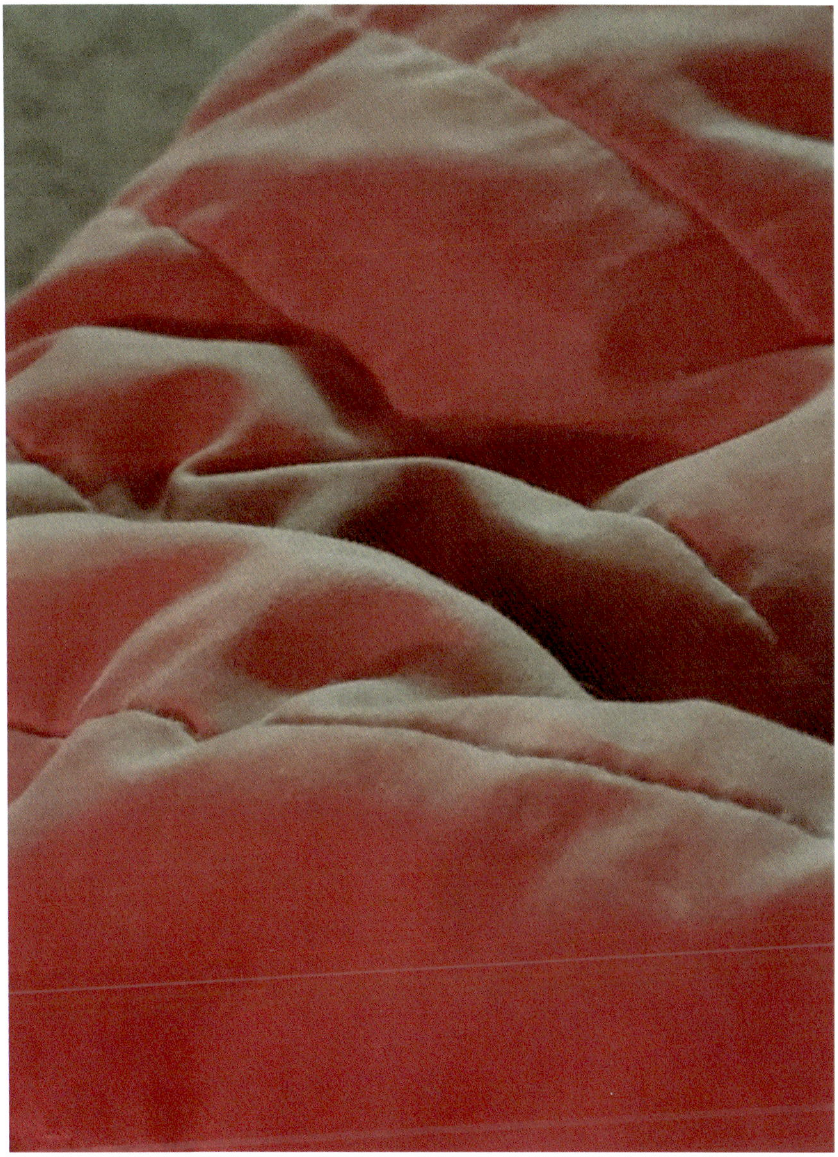

↑ Posted by u/Zenb**** 4 days ago

128

↓

Bruhhhh

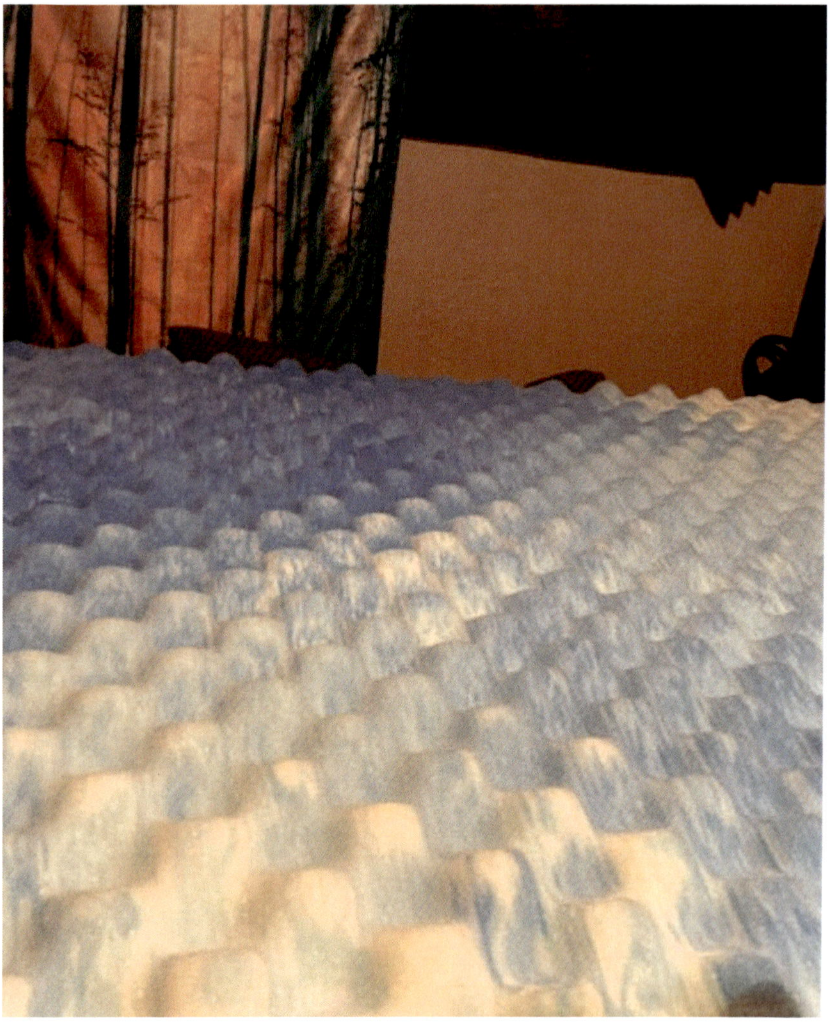

Posted by u/an_e**** 4 days ago

178

Trippy veggies

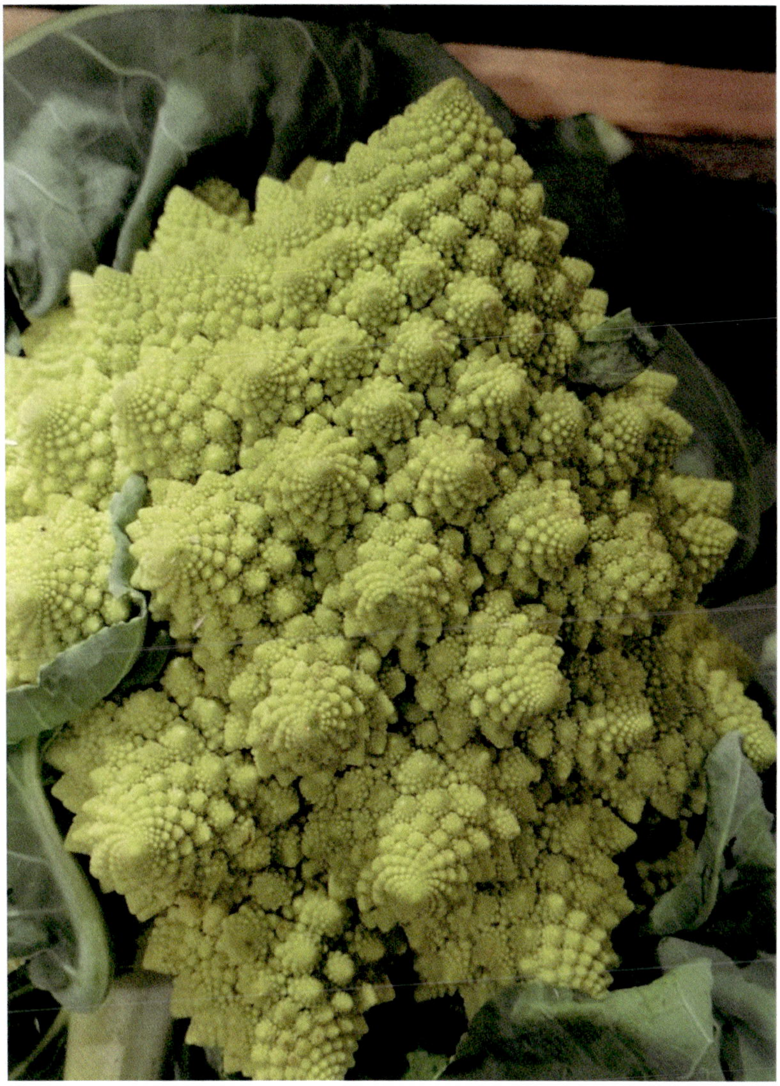

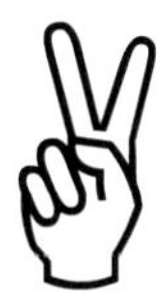

Published by Unknown Unknowns.

Unknown Unknowns are books written by ghost-writers, algorithms, and other automatic means. These volumes consider how computers and artificial intelligence influence language when processes like compiling and surveillance replace original writing and observation.

More information at unknownunknowns.org.